BODIED

unclaimed
ideas

01

Kedela wer kalyakoorl ngalak Whadjuk boodjak yak.

The Art Gallery of Western Australia acknowledges the traditional custodians of the lands on which we work, the Whadjuk Noongar people in Boorloo, Perth. We honour and pay respect to community Elders and to their ancestors who survived and cared for this Country. The Gallery recognises that sovereignty was never ceded.

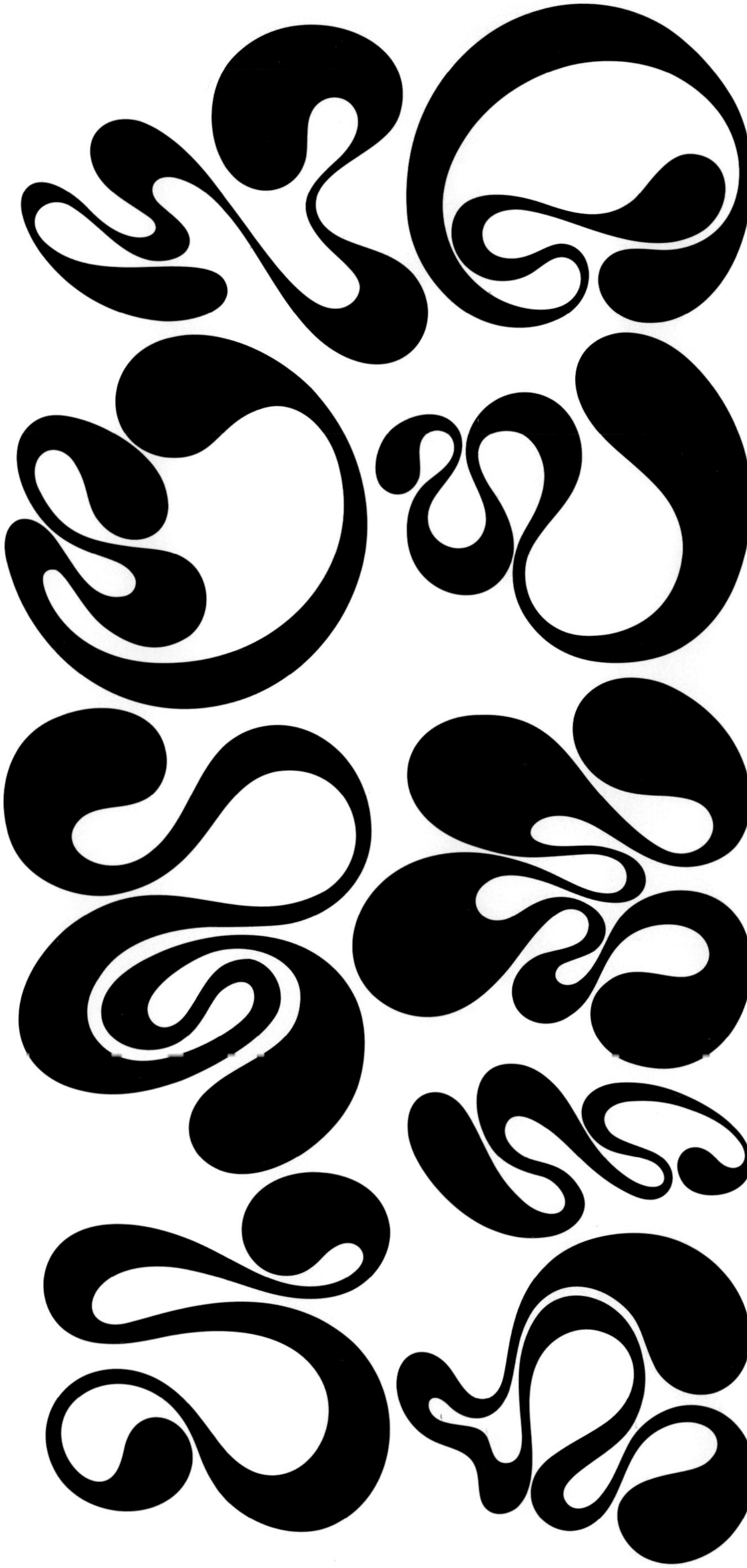

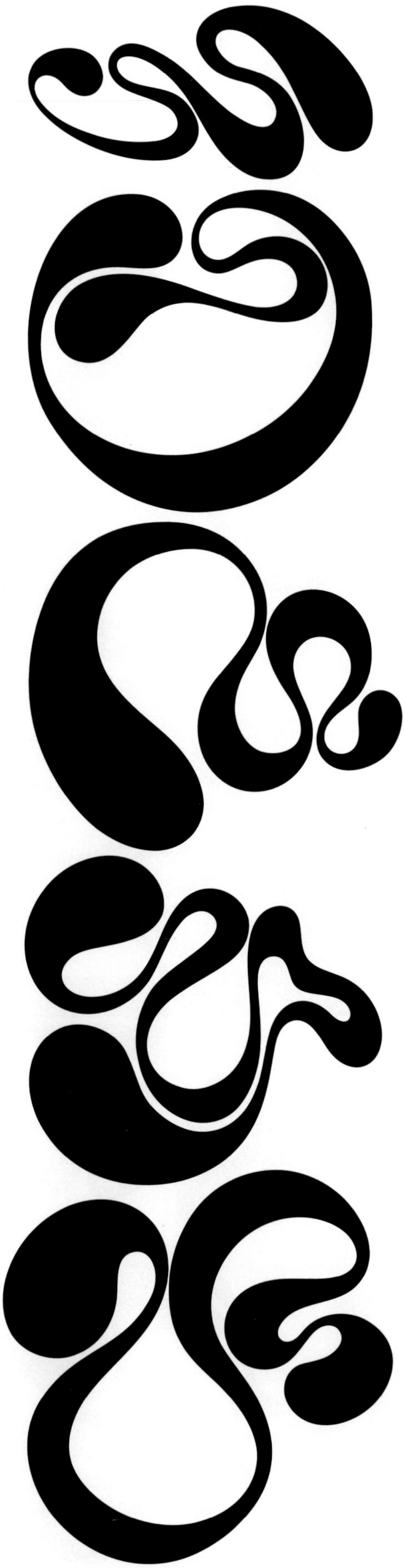

BODIED is the first title in our new publication series 'Unclaimed Ideas' and the first project jointly conceived by The Art Gallery of Western Australia (AGWA) and the Simon Lee Foundation Institute of Contemporary Asian Art (SLF ICAA). Created as a series of paperback readers, 'Unclaimed Ideas' collects essays and interviews by leading voices and undiscovered talents who change the way we understand artistic practice and its relationship to the most critical issues in the world today.

Led by Rachel Ciesla, SLF ICAA is a major new creative and curatorial initiative at AGWA. Generously supported by the Simon Lee Foundation, this visionary project will enrich and deepen AGWA's connections with contemporary art practices and cultural thinking in Asia and its diaspora communities. Through an integrated program of research, digital projects, exhibitions and collection development, it will present new and notable Asian artists, and foster the exchange of art and ideas throughout Western Australia and the wider region in partnership with our global institutional peers.

BODIED unites an internationally diverse group of artists who, in positioning the body at the centre of their practice, explore how our physical forms are shaped by the social worlds around us. The project began life as an exhibition at AGWA in December 2020 which featured the work of Gordon Bennett, Cheryl Donegan, Alin Huma and Cheiko Kawaguchi, Jani Ruscica, Kawita Vatanajyankur, and Wong Ping. The exhibition was an open response to many of the issues of that moment including social inequality, social atomisation and surveillance. Staged within a section of the Gallery that was once police offices and law courts, it expounded a dialogue between the artists' creative propositions, the moment of their display, and the colonial legacy and context of the space in which they were exhibited.

In this book, curators Rachel Ciesla and Robert Cook present a collection of interviews with exhibiting artists. The interviews explore the arcs and parameters of each artist's practice as they intersect with current changing political and cultural contexts. The artist interviews are accompanied by a reproduction of Ian McLean's essay on Gordon Bennett, 'Shadow Time' – originally written for the 1996 Adelaide Biennial of Australian Art which also presented Bennett's video *Performance with Object for the Expiation of Guilt (Apple Premiere Mix),* 1995 – as well as a new text by Bahar Sayed and an introduction by Rachel Ciesla and Robert Cook. By foregrounding the artists' voices, the book reveals the thoughtfulness of their practices in material, conceptual and social terms. Each artist positions their work as an open inquiry into the world, buoyed by an incredibly generous critical spirit.

The release of this book is timed to coincide with the premiere of two new works commissioned by AGWA and SLF ICAA: Kawita Vatanajyankur's *Mental Machine: Labour in the Self Economy,* 2022, a live durational performance, made in collaboration with Pat Pataranutaporn from Fluid Interface at MIT Media Lab, which will be staged in the Gallery's lower concourse; and a mural by Wong Ping, his first site-specific work in Australia, which will be installed across AGWA's foyer. These projects reflect our commitment to supporting contemporary artists and offering audiences some of the most inspiring art of today. This publication series was conceived from the outset as a means of connecting people with the ways artists are mobilising themselves to think through the social, cultural and personal fallout of the political and environmental crises that increasingly define the current moment. In this spirit, SLF ICAA will continue to find ways to explore multiple art histories beyond North America and Western Europe, creating new conversations founded on curiosity, possibility and – most importantly – connection.

AGWA and SLF ICAA would like to acknowledge the assistance of a number of individuals and organisations that helped make this project possible. Most importantly, our sincere thanks go to the artists for their enthusiastic support of this project and for generously giving their time throughout the interview and editing process: Wong Ping and his representatives Lorraine Kiang, Edouard Malingue and Ryan Lai; Cheryl Donegan; Alin Huma and Cheiko Kawaguchi; Jani Ruscica; and Kawita Vatanajyankur. Thanks also to Leanne Bennett for her gracious support in providing information about Gordon Bennett's work. Thanks to Bahar Sayed for her nuanced text in this publication, and to the designers, Una X and Marco Dalle Fratte, who enthusiastically agreed to support this project from the outset. Their adventurous aesthetic sensibility signals SLF ICAA's focus on showcasing the most innovative ideas of our time.

AGWA would like to acknowledge the editors and co-curators, Rachel Ciesla and Robert Cook. We also extend our thanks to AGWA's Board and its Chair Janet Holmes à Court, The Art Gallery of Western Australia Foundation, and fellow Trustees of the Simon Lee Foundation for their significant cultural investment in supporting this initiative and its contribution to Western Australia's vibrant artistic community. This will enable us to strengthen our connections to art, artists and each other; and to deepen our understanding of the world in order to help us imagine new futures.

Colin Walker
Director,
Art Gallery of
Western Australia

Orion Lee
Trustee, Simon
Lee Foundation

Medium in mediums: Exhibition notes 8
Rachel Ciesla & Robert Cook

Shadow Time 12
an McLean on Gordon Bennett

Interviews 49
Cheryl Donegan
Alin Huma
Jani Ruscica
Kawita Vatanajyankur
Wong Ping

Hoping for a Good Life Everybody is Exhausted 93
Bahar Sayed

Mediums in mediums: Exhibition notes

Rachel Ciesla
& Robert Cook

BODIED was an intuitive alignment in the bounded shape of a small exhibition.

Set back. Taking place over a southern hemisphere summer: late 2020, early 2021.

Performative, physically-focused video works and printed matter looped and lay in galleries that were once the colony's police law courts. Spaces that were not backgrounds or backdrops but politico-phenomenological presences.

Vacated in the 1970s. Exhibition spaces from 1995. Retaining their heritage features.

The architecture convincingly manifests a set of systems and techniques: of judgement, population control, incarceration.

As if to rub this in, there are no doors or sound blocks between the spaces. From some positions a viewer might hear the works speaking between architectural and historical thresholds.

(We both remember a crossing of voices)

Registering in the way a river can sound, binding and unbinding.

Re-constituting, while in motion, a listener might patch together a peripheral perception of moving image fragments in the way a migraine begins. Prior to flickering out a patterned gesturing between the constrained body and the decreated self.

This is all very abstract. But it reflects a possible held or un-held moment of passage.

Towards coherence. When a viewer attends to the duration of individual works and the urgent and lingering questions that create the repercussions of a single focal point/person/point.

As the shape of the exhibition becomes recognisable there is always this kind of lapping and tugging.

Something that, in Kristeva's semiotics, is an orientation of voices.
Voices that remain even as the tide rises.

We see Kawaguchi in performance, in a book, opened out, in a case, standing, with a mop of black hair; as Bennett, on a small television screen, veers from a history that might careen out of control to the point where the television falls to the ground at the same time as Ruscica's letter 'F' announces itself as a word. A punctuating velocity.

Attention and focus, then meaning. Or meaning, then attention and focus. Shapes, binding. Binding shapes. Punctured and still, moving still.

BODIED's gestures were constantly drawing us towards interrelated formations that buoy and crush and release being and becoming.

Straight-faced, we might 'call me by your name' them: language, media, fashion, gender, sex, race.

As if to speak shorthand in aftershock. In full view of tremors generated by power and biology, culture and nature that we can share and feel when they are located as artworks labouring.

Some phrases about how works worked: 'charting', 'rebelling against', 'coping with', 'sublimating the affective', 'adopting critical strategies', and 'stances', 'the platform for new and better modes of being bodies together'.

True but too boosterish? It wasn't yet end times.
What seems clearer now. It isn't yet end times.

End, not-end. There is a negative and a positive space, and moment, to see, to address the mechanism; and this calms things down a little.

Donegan on Zoom as her winter closed in: 'I did my self-expression in the midst of this situation that I'd set up. It was almost like the situation had to occur for the expression to occur. For me, that truly was the takeaway for moving forward with how to make art.'

The 'situation' is her 1994 video *Head*. In which she becomes a medium, acting out what was possible within its constraints, within a series of other mediums: patriarchy, video art, painting, gravity.

Vatanajyankur, situated. Trains herself to accommodate the labour. Enduring her work that makes her the tool in another work.

A medium in a series of other mediums: patriarchy, performance art, capitalism, hygiene, gravity.

Expanding the edge of the bearable, her practice is practicing.

Tolerances. Accommodations. To make discipline her discipline.
This task registers as an affront with its own gravity.
We thought the title 'BODIED' might claim this.
There are many ways of being taken out.

In Ruscica's *Human Flesh*, an experiment staged within the human operating system.

That zone of intimate extimacy. Biology and culture twin. Though we speak, are spoken of and to, in division.

Capacities and devices twin. Forgetting and intention being one and the same in the performance of the word. The you that is carried out of yourself by yourself.

Has its own situational energy.
As Bennett's whip rises while falling to crack and straighten.

The lash is a medium in a medium: colonialism, performance art, expressionism, irony, gravity.

Bennett, acting into the mechanism that acts on him, and in which he saw an end that was not accommodation, tolerance.

We realise these are not end points for Donegan or Vatanajyankur either.
Or for Ruscica; the pushing ahead of plosive utterances.

They require some kind of preparation.

A run up, a will to destroy the mechanism as one trusts in it. See Sayed on this.

To be released from the condition of the medium in the medium.
To walk out of its cinema, the fibre of its storytelling.

Huma and Kawaguchi play this out in *IOU*. An idea of energy in mind, or drive. What does one do with a camera, with a verge, with a photographer, with a performer, with a goldfish in a plastic bag? With a fridge. Heating to cool, as Huma tells us. Cooling to heat too.

The work that is not labour but action cancels the functionality of nihilism and cynicism in favour of other functions.

An aphorism a day.

We can see and diagnose this widely: the work is the work of the mechanism that enacts a separation of cause and effect while causing and affecting.

An exchange value: IOU. I owe you.

To spell it out, Wong's *Stop Peeping* is pulled towards exchange, frisson (that skirts it).

The medium of attraction, the medium of perversion.

The work working on erecting a bridge from the privacy of the fetish to the...

Over the ...

This working is not meant to work.
Satisfaction is a failure.

You cannot remain aware of this. Try it. Try always thinking of this. Try creeping around town as a low-rent Wittgenstein for once in your soggy life!

The mechanism Wong shapes and submits himself to is the agent of forgetting by way of observation.

That it might be bound, shaped. This forgetting is looking. That leaves your desire spread across your body. And hanging. There.

How far are we from the notion of a predicament really?

It is hard to know until it has bodied us.
And then, to enter the loop again.

Or something else?

Gordon Bennett

Gordon Bennett's video *Performance with Object for the Expiation of Guilt (Apple Premiere Mix)*, 1995, was produced just after Bennett had attended summer school classes in video-making. The work shows the artist in a blockish black suit wielding a bullwhip which he cracks near a black coffin-shaped box that has been made to the dimensions of his own body. During this performance, a series of words denigrating Indigenous people is projected behind him to form an enveloping scene of lurid and chaotic violence. Making connections between the treatment of workers on rural properties in Australia, abstract expressionism and the whirr of the stockman's whip, Bennett assumes the ambiguous position of acting out the violence, and being a subject to it, in a loop that implicates unbounded expressiveness. His mourning is active and resistive, pushing back inwards and outwards to reveal the situational workings of the system as it enfolds its subjects.

Gordon Bennett was born in Monto, Queensland in 1955. He lived and worked in Meanjin/Brisbane until his untimely death in 2014. One of Australia's most prominent and critically engaged artists, Bennett achieved significant national and international recognition during his thirty year career. He was represented in biennials in Sydney (1992, 2000, 2008), Venice (1995), Kwangju (2000), Shanghai (2000), Prague (2005) and Berlin (2014), as well as the prestigious Documenta 13 in Kassel (2012).

Shadow Time

an McLean
on Gordon Bennett

Shadow Time

Ian McLean

Colonialist ideology has so upset the ethical basis of subjecthood that the subject and its arrangements of identity and genealogies are on the verge of collapse. The vanguard of this new post-subjectivity are the subaltern and indigenous peoples who, through colonialism, were made strangers in their own homes. If their only compensation was the promise of a new home offered by a postcolonial future, this promise, Homi Bhabha observed, is never fulfilled. The postcolonial home remains unhomed.[1]

Coloniality plunges migrants and indigenous populations into the same undifferentiated space of loss from which they must refigure their identities. In colonial societies all parties, indigenous, settler and diasporic, eventually become supplementary to an origin or home which no longer exists. This experience of loss also overtook the colonisers when an alienating modernity transformed Europe's former centres into the frontier zones of collapsed differences we call postmodernity. In this sense, the effects of European colonialism, which are 500 years old, appear quintessentially postmodernist. Even the economic and political strategies of colonialism – appropriation and colonisation – have become the aesthetic devices of postmodernism. Thus it might seem that we are all in the same boat. Unhinged from our histories and traditions by the deluge of coloniality and modernity, we, like Noah in his ark, herald new genealogies that take no account of previous differences.

If the cultural differences which once meant so much in discourses of identity are now dissolving into a tolerant shadowless multicultural regime of globalised cultural diversity that threatens the very concept of indigeneity, what has become of difference, of the Other? To all appearances, it has been negated, leaving a world which, says Meaghan Morris, is 'shadowless, depthless, invasive'.[2] Even the genealogies and histories which once nourished our sense of self have, relates Morris, been substituted by what Fredric Jameson called 'pop history'[3] – a flat disembodied post-history, like those period dramas which imagine the past and future, the here and there, as so many simulacra of Hollywood.

If the stereotypes of pop history are the limits of today's historical imagination, Gordon Bennett takes these limits as a starting point to be exceeded – or in Morris's words (about her own work), 'as a point of departure for asking questions' that will trace the 'shadows on the landscape'[4] of Australia's pop history. Bennett's strategy for picturing such shadows is to locate difference in the midst of postmodernist indifference. In his computer enhanced video *Performance with Object for the Expiation of Guilt (Apple Premier Mix) 1995*, the postcolonial 'self' is represented in the dissolving image of his own body being pursued by its shadow, and surrounded by a barrage of slogans that exemplify the pop history of Australian colonialism. If, like postmodernism, the shifting space of this work elevates liminality, loss and contingency to an ontology, it also challenges the a-moral turn of postmodern (post) subjectivity by locating the fractured postcolonial 'self' in a genealogy of colonial semiologies. By unpacking the binary patterns or differences of these semiologies, Bennett hopes to return to the politics of otherness enacted by colonialism.

Bennett eschews those postmodernist mythologies of subversion and transcendence that aim to start again without history, for the more pragmatic purpose of staying in the game, of negotiating not negating positions.[5] The difference is an ethical one, and one that locates his hybrid aesthetic in the syncretic practices of subaltern colonial cultures (which used collage and appropriation as a strategy of translation well before it found a place in Western (post)modernism). While modernist collage and postmodernist appropriation aim to decentre the subject through a politics of simultaneity (de-historicised meaning) and negation (of origins), the colonised subject is already decentred, already an object of negation. For subaltern communities, a collaged hybrid subjectivity is an everyday means of survival which negotiates and centres decentred subject positions. It is literally a means of making an identity by juxtaposing and crossing over the differences of an excess of roots, rather than, as in (post)modernism, a symbolic means of transforming an excess of roots into a rootlessness, into a negation or loss which might clear the ground for a new future.

The ethics of postcolonial and postmodern collage hinge on the agency each accords to the self and the Other. Jameson has shown how the hybrid contingencies of life in late capitalism lends itself to an ethics of indifference, of an absence of the Other, which is no ethics at all. Here difference is so pervasive that its repetitions perversely create a culture of sameness in which subjectivity becomes oceanic, structurally void and so without agency. There is diversity without difference, pastiche without parody. Binaries disappear, shadows dissolve. However, like shadows cast by a full moon, Bennett's Aboriginal genealogy constantly crosses his path. Thus his art is not a simple story of one side against the other (as is most colonial discourses), or of the collapse of one into the other (as with postmodernism), but of the haunting of difference (or the Other) in identity.

For Carl Jung, not only do each of us have an alter-ego, unconscious or shadow which projects our fears onto others, but each society has a collective shadow that is expressed in the mythologies of that society, usually as grotesque forms. As with Jungian analysis, the object of Bennett's work is not to expel these shadows, but to know them.[6] In *Performance with Object for the Expiation of Guilt*, a performance video piece first made in February 1994, and re-edited in January 1995 as *Performance with Object for the Expiation of Guilt (Apple Premier Mix)*, Bennett performs dressed in a black suit, his face wrapped in a white bandage like the invisible man, whipping a black box built to the dimensions of his own body, abusing it with racist words. On one level the whip is a simile for the violent gaze of Western metaphysics and its language of binary enclosures. But Bennett fetishistic ritual of sacrifice and atonement renders ambiguous the binary relations of subject and object that such exercises usually imply. Instead of collapsing these binary relations into an arena of cultural diversity, Bennett maps a space of difference into which he falls. Here ethics is not transcended by a politics of multi-culturalism and historical forgetfullness, but returned in the circularity of every thought and action. As his self paces between its constitutive parts of invisible body and its alter-forms of box and shadow, the shadow mimics his every move, returning his objectifying abuse to its origin in the politics of otherness.

End Notes

1. 'Unhomeliness' wrote Bhabha, 'is the condition of extra-territorial and cross-cultural initiations.' (Homi Bhabha, 'Introduction', *The Location of Culture*, Routledge, London 1994, p. 9)
2. Meaghan Morris, 'Panorama The Live, The Dead and The Living', *Island in the Stream.*, ed Paul Foss, Pluto Press, Leichardt, 1988, p.163.

   However the postmodern world is pervasive rather than invasive. In this totalising postsubject regime of post-modernism, the concept of invasion is anachronistic because there are no points of resistance.
3. Fredric Jameson, Postmodernism, or the Cultural Logic of Late Capitalism, *New Left Review,* 146,1984, p.71.
4. Ibid., p.166.
5. See Bhabha's distinction between negotiation and negationin, 'The Commitment to Theory', *The Location of Culture,* op. cit. p.25.
6. Bennett's clearest statement on his debt to Jung's ideas is 'On shadows (of my former self)', which accompanied his Septemeber 1995 exhibition at Sutton Galleries, Melbourne.

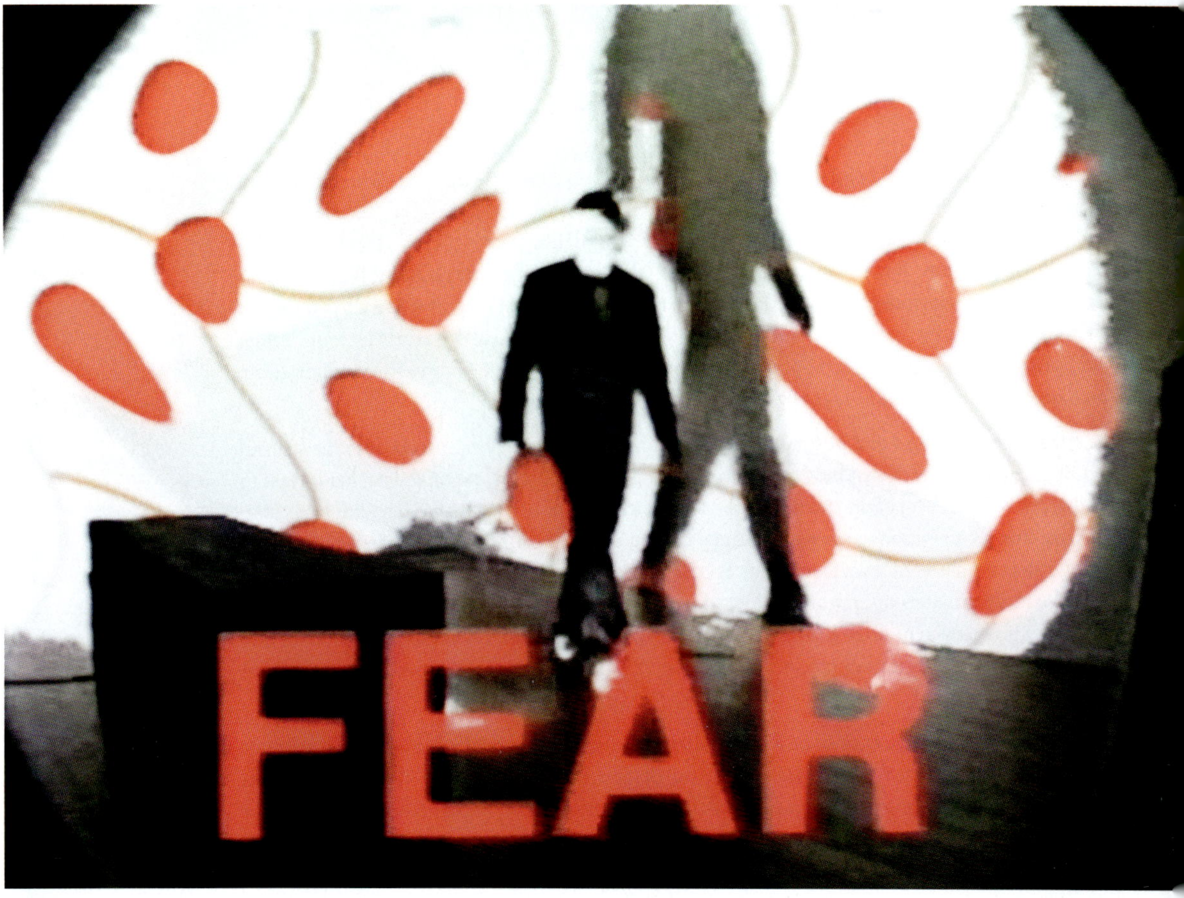

[01]

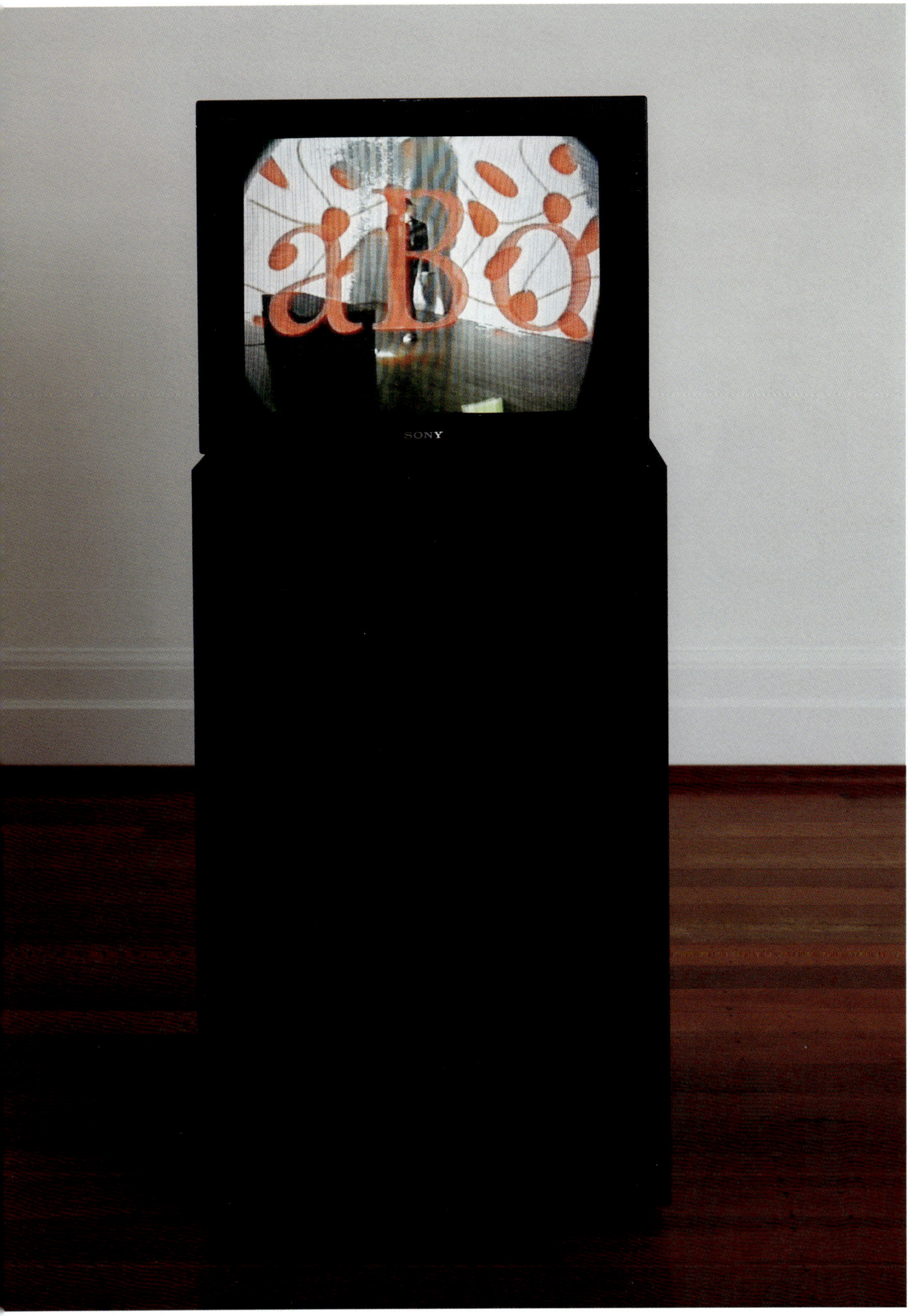

[02]

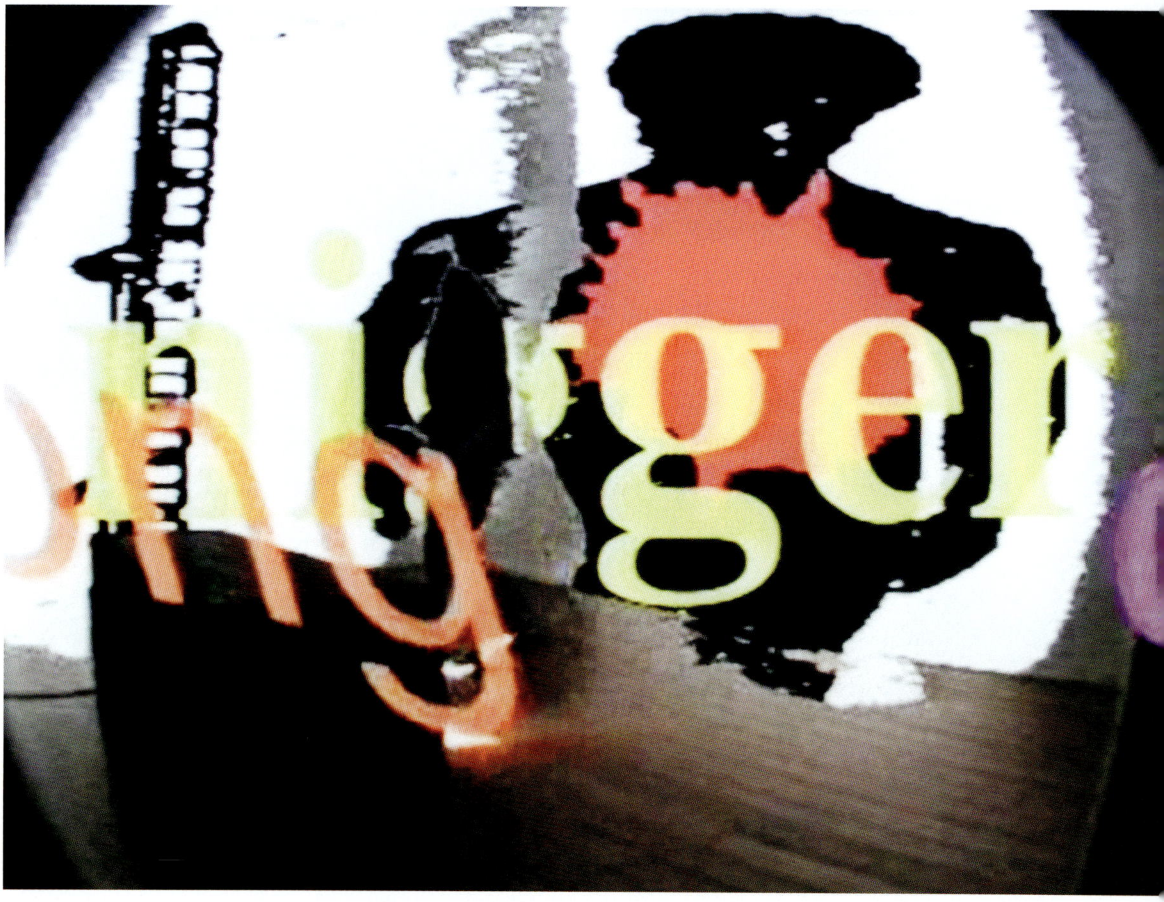

(03)

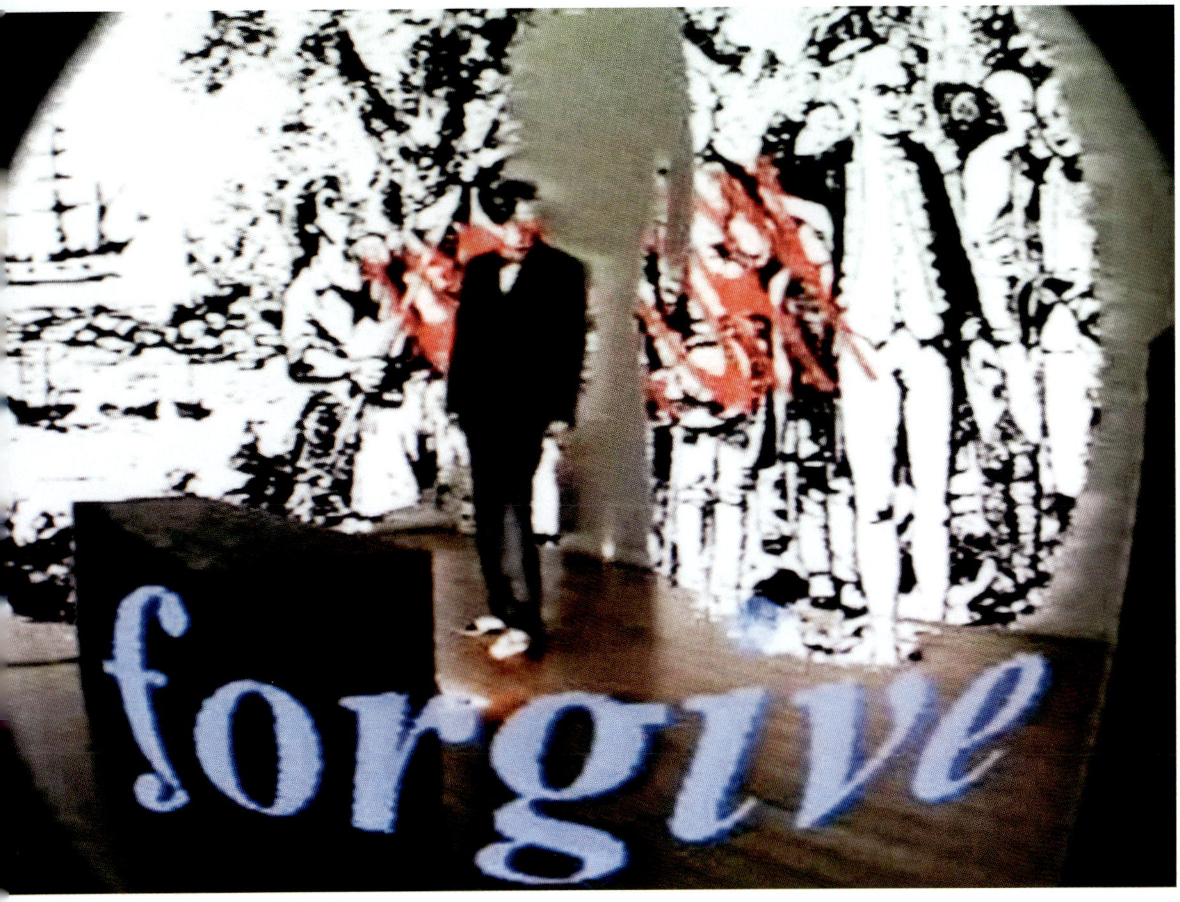

[04]

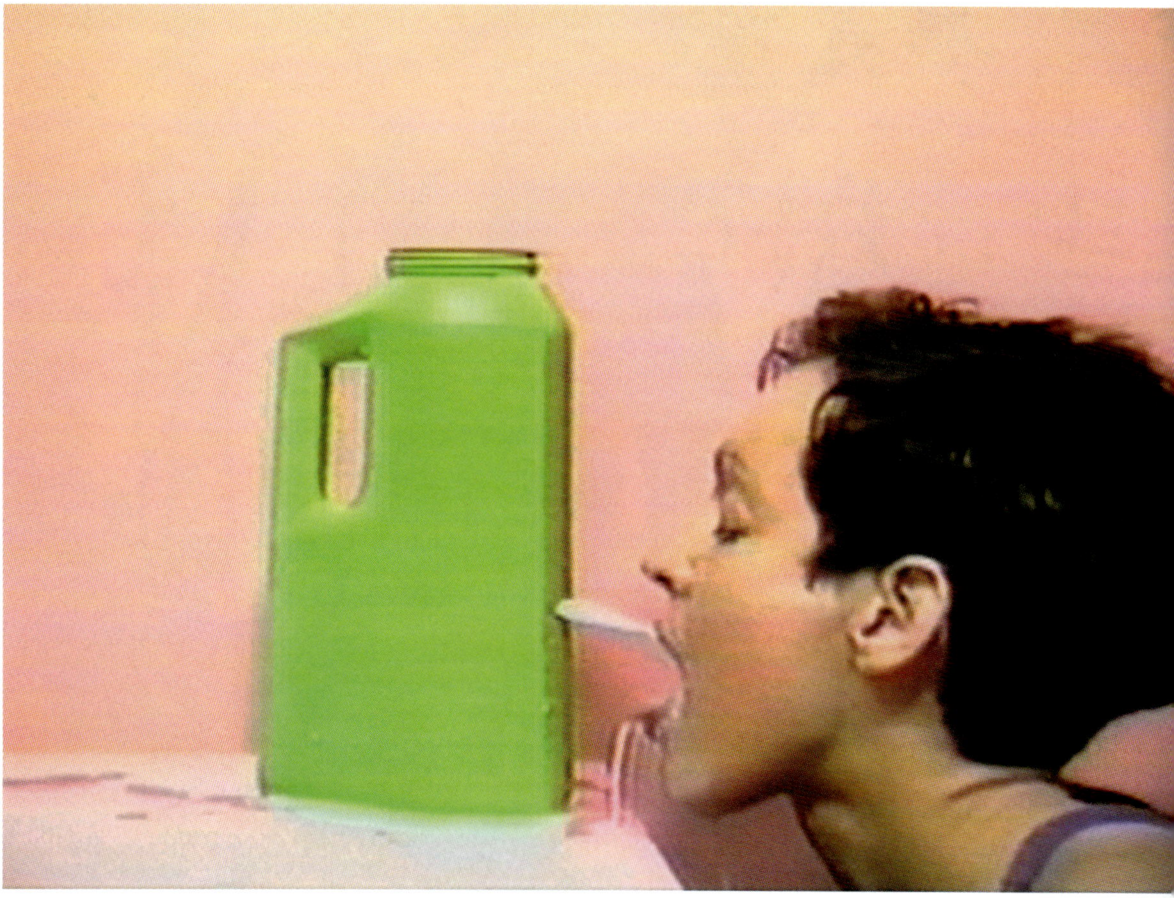

[05]

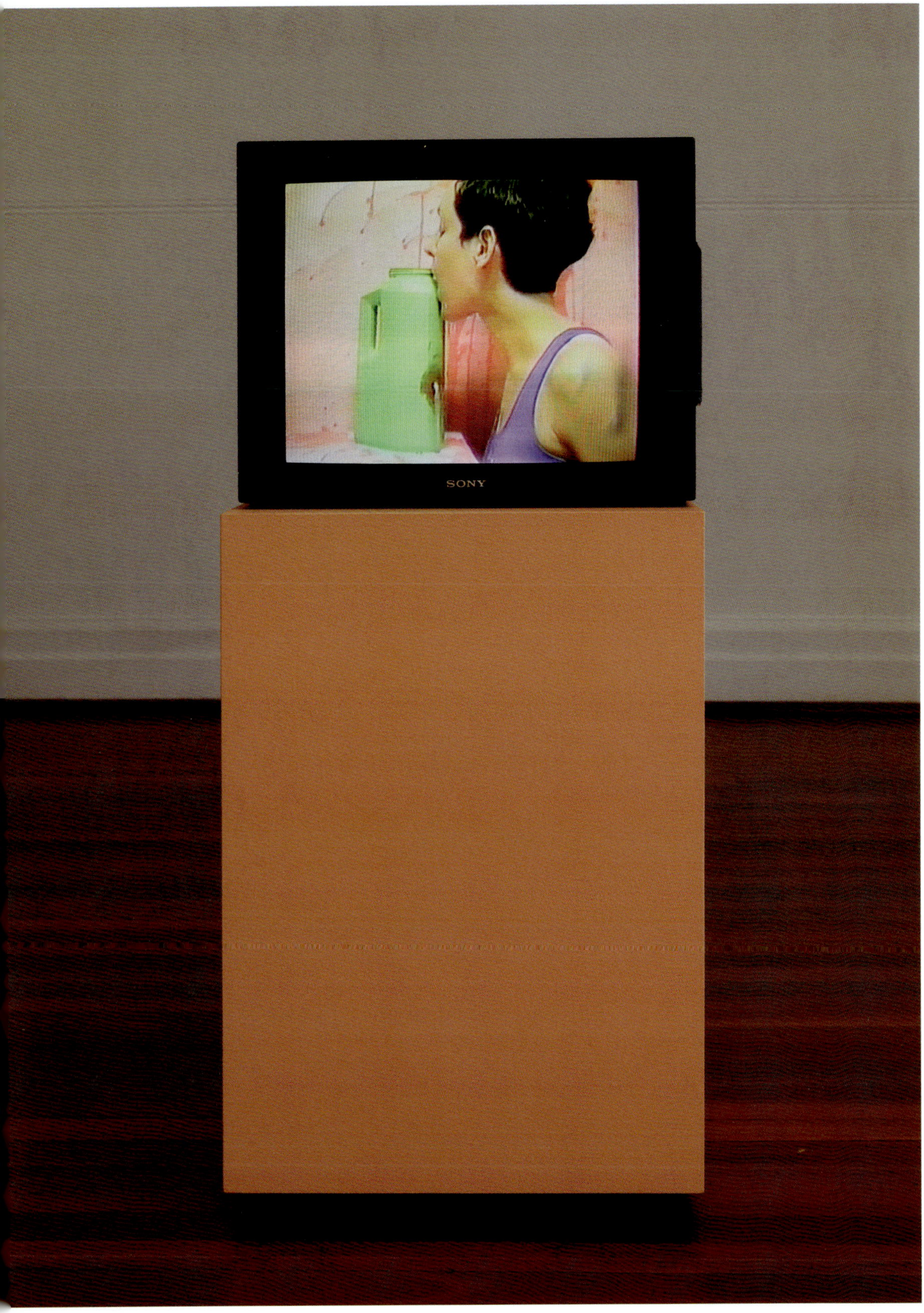

(06)

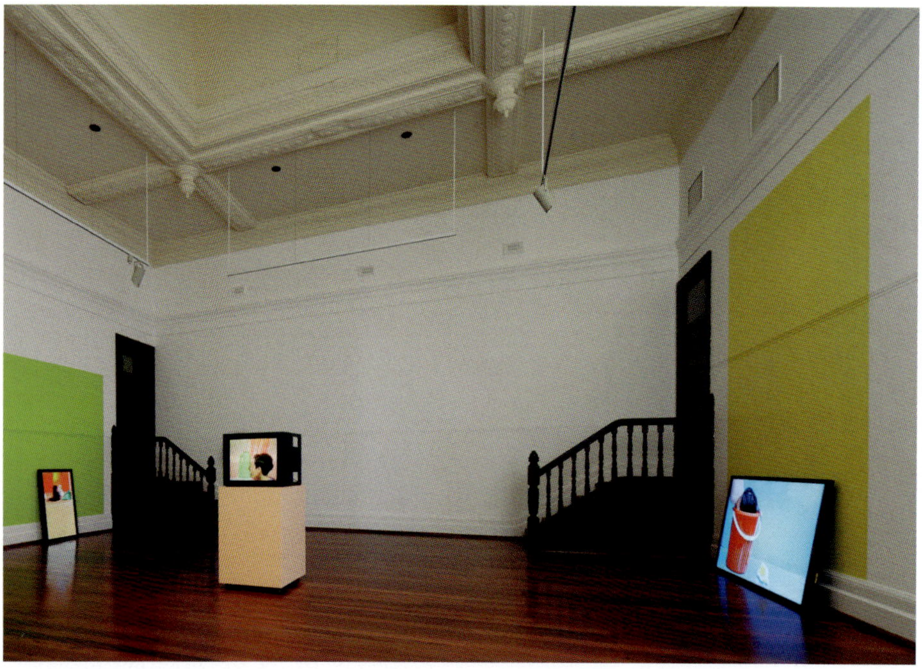

(07)

(08)

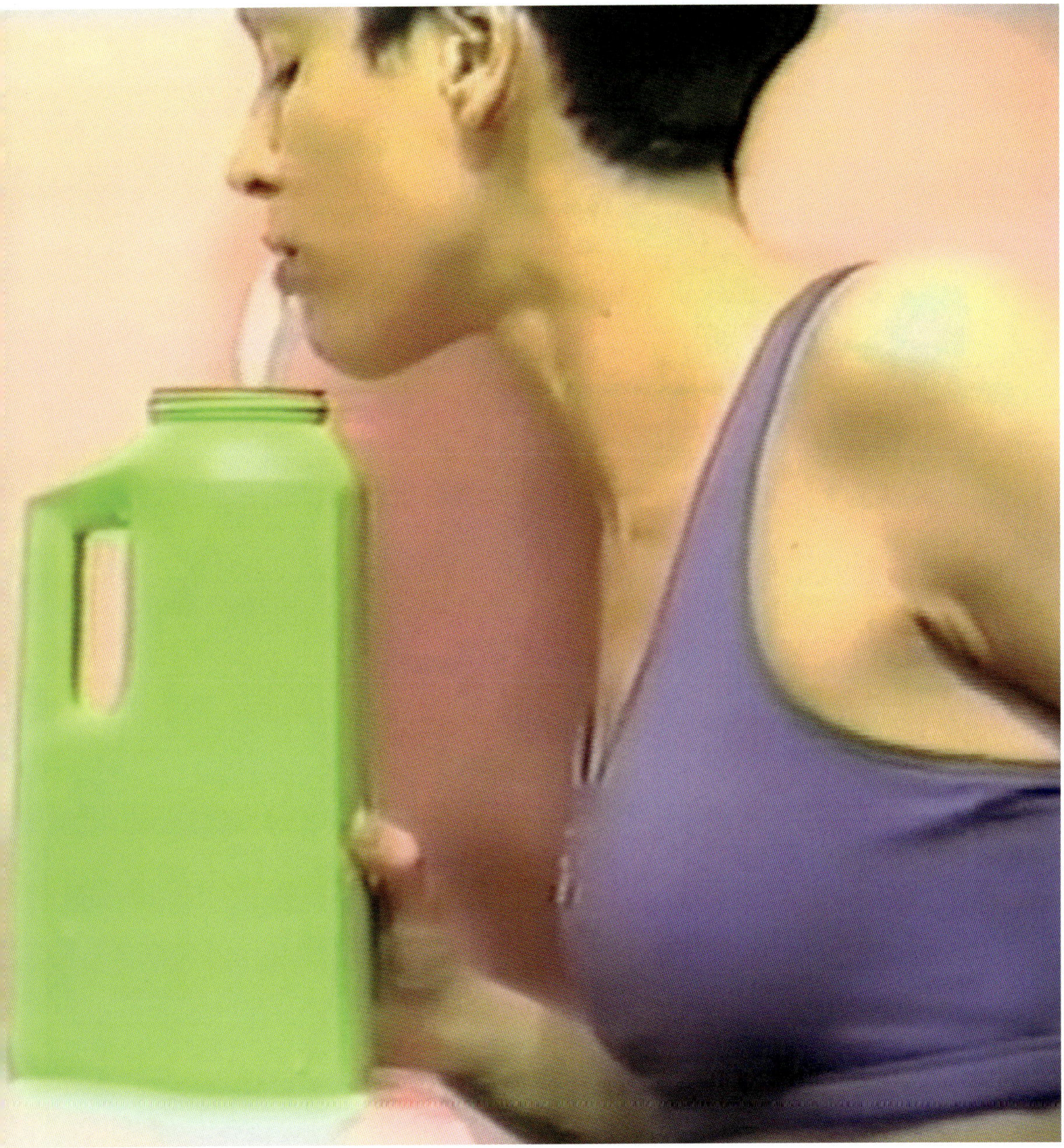

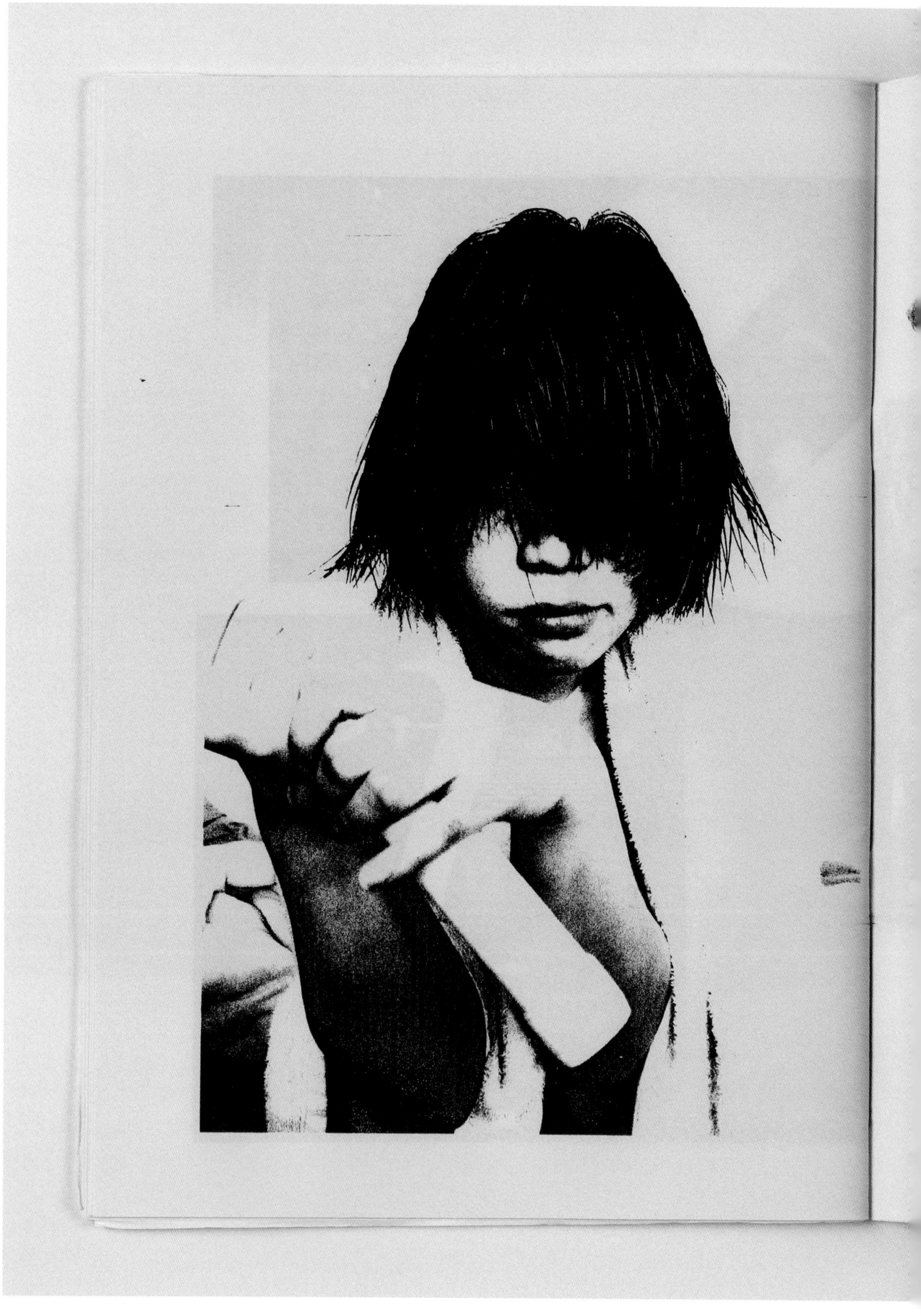

(09)

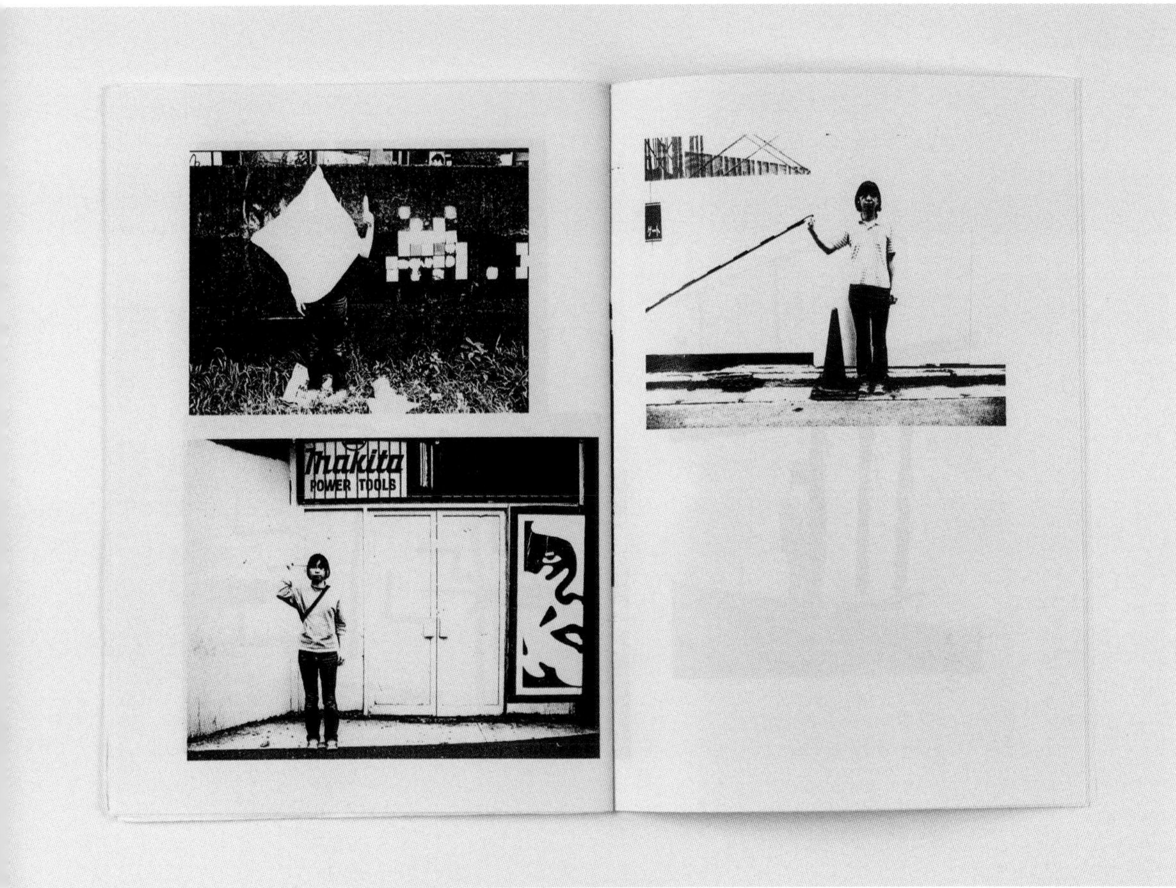

〔10〕

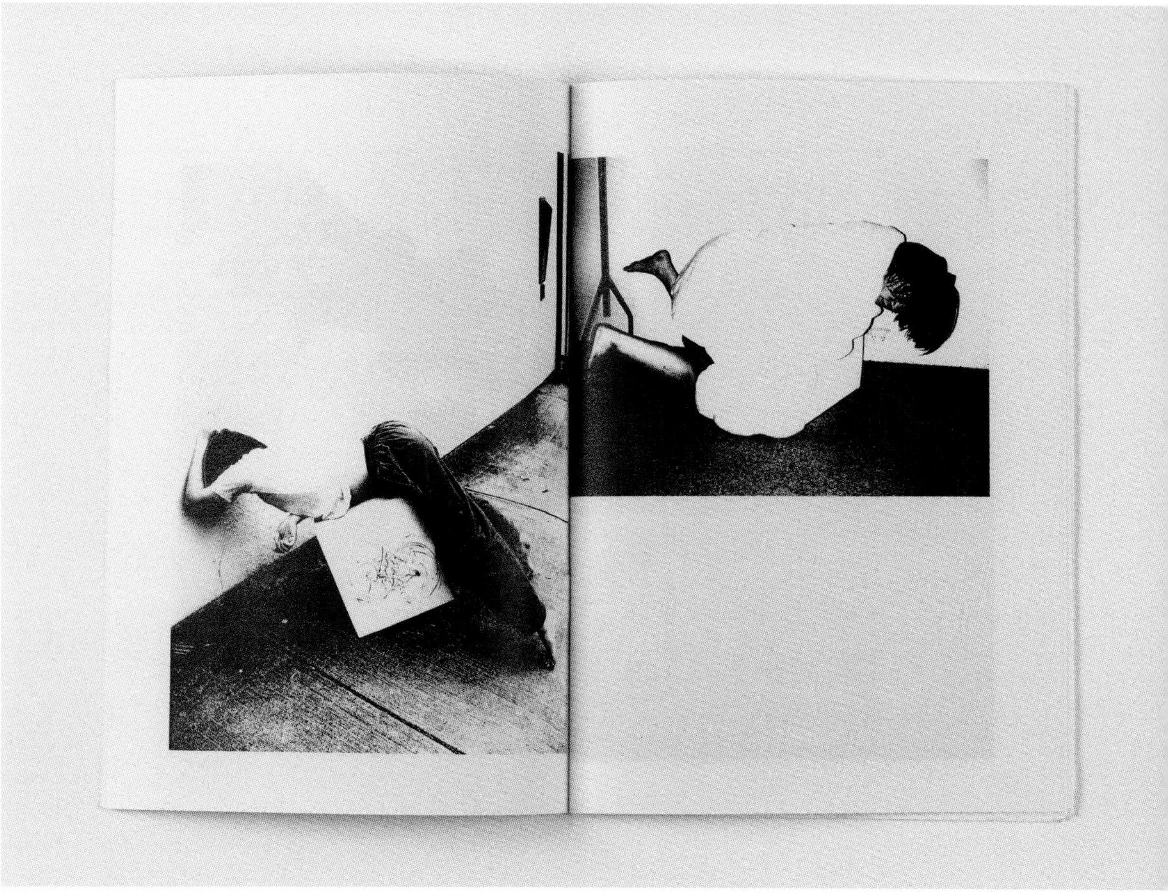

(11)

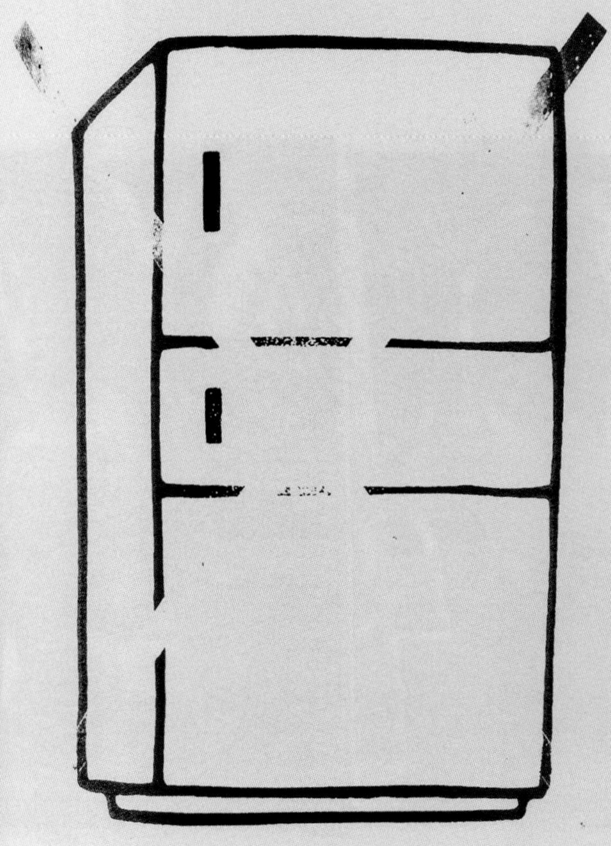

冷蔵庫

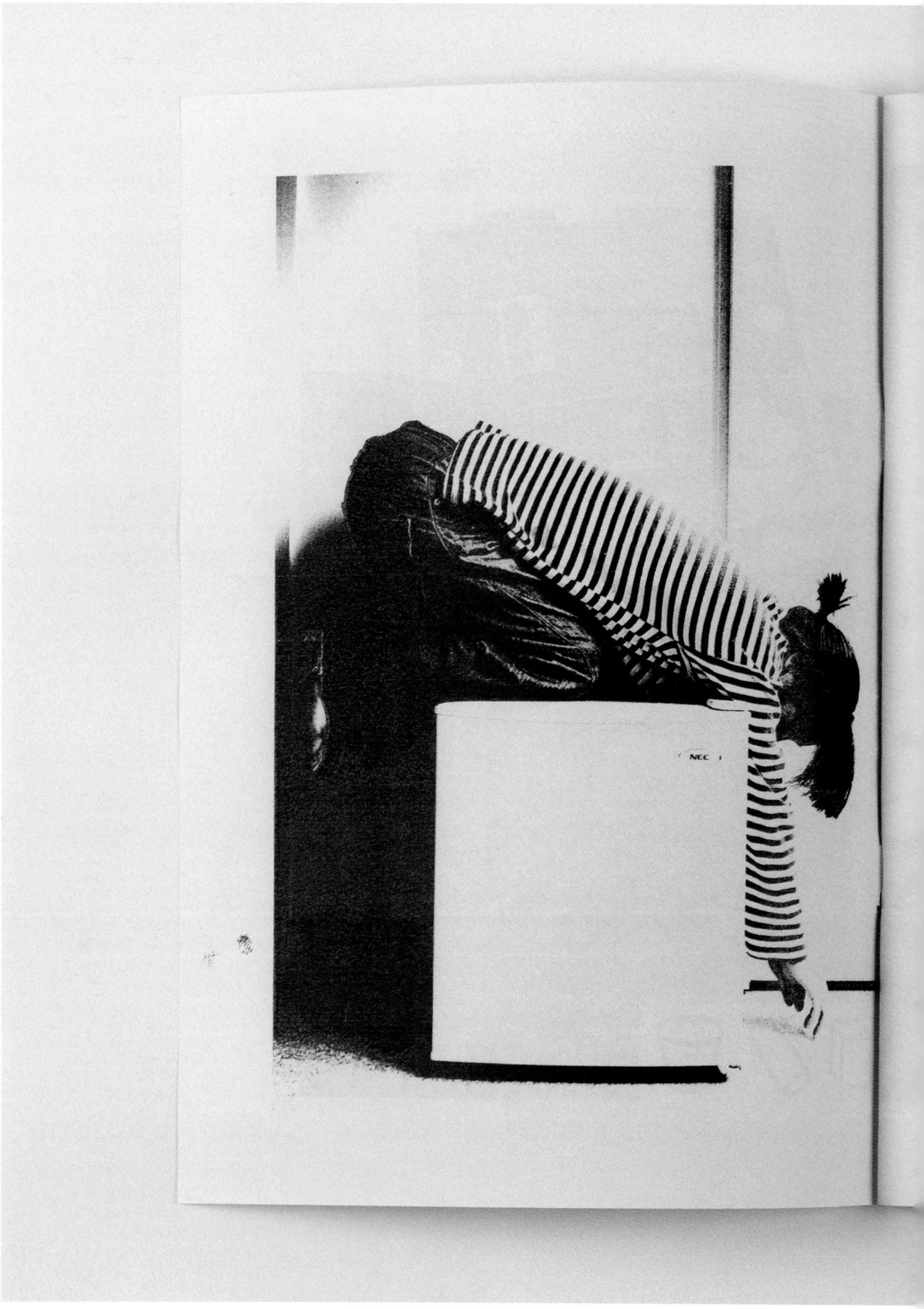

(13)

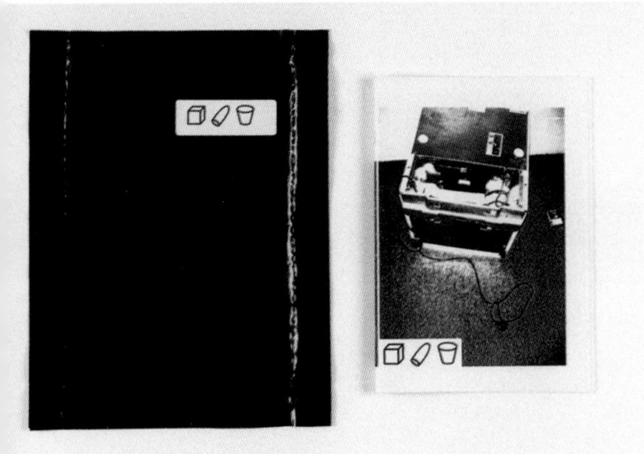

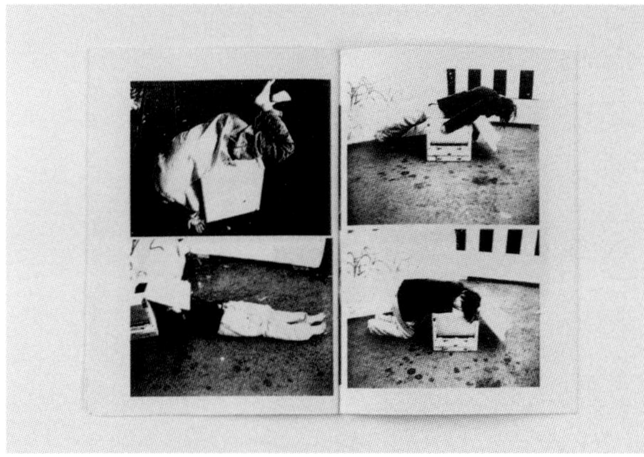

(14)

(15)

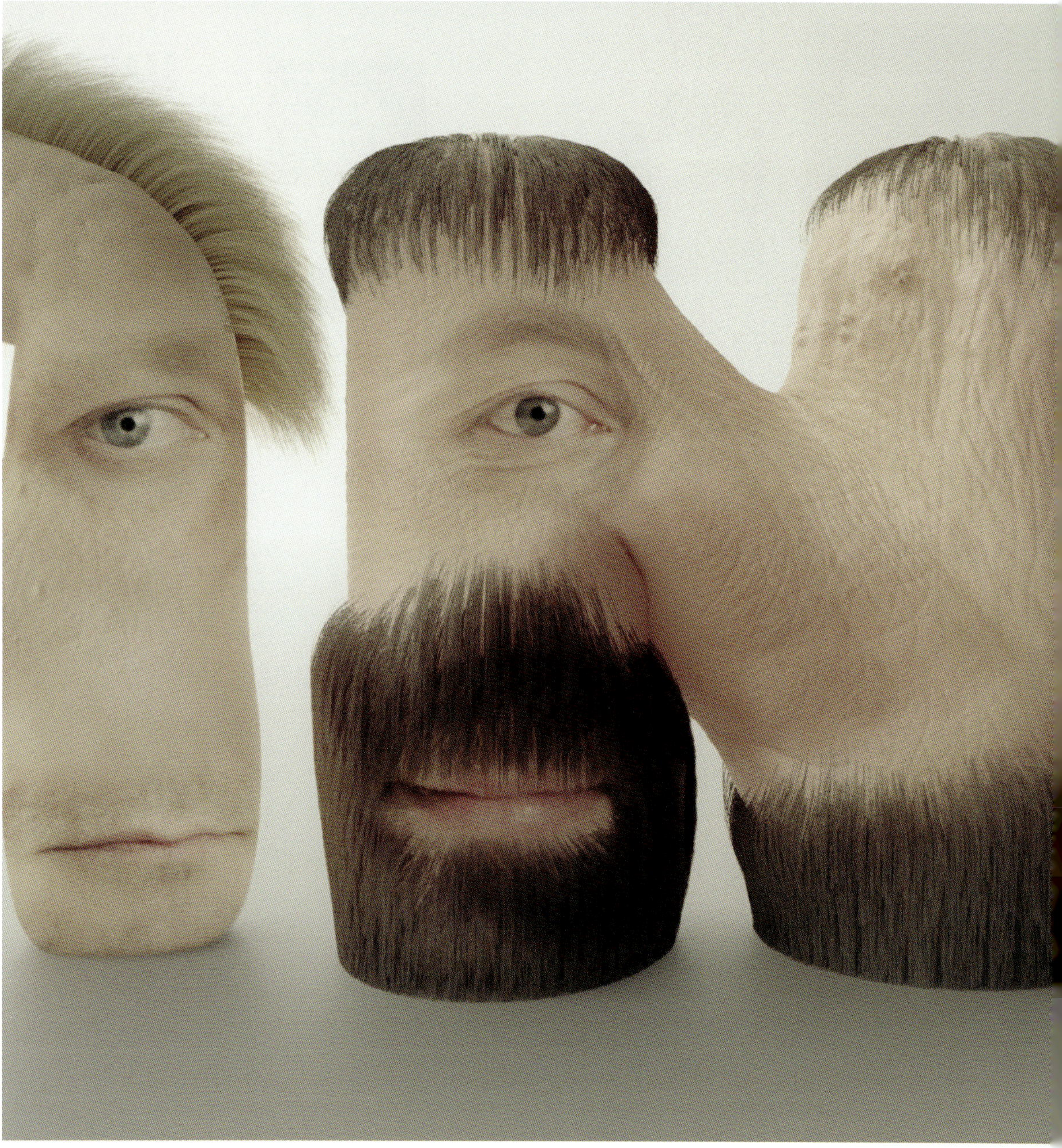

(16)

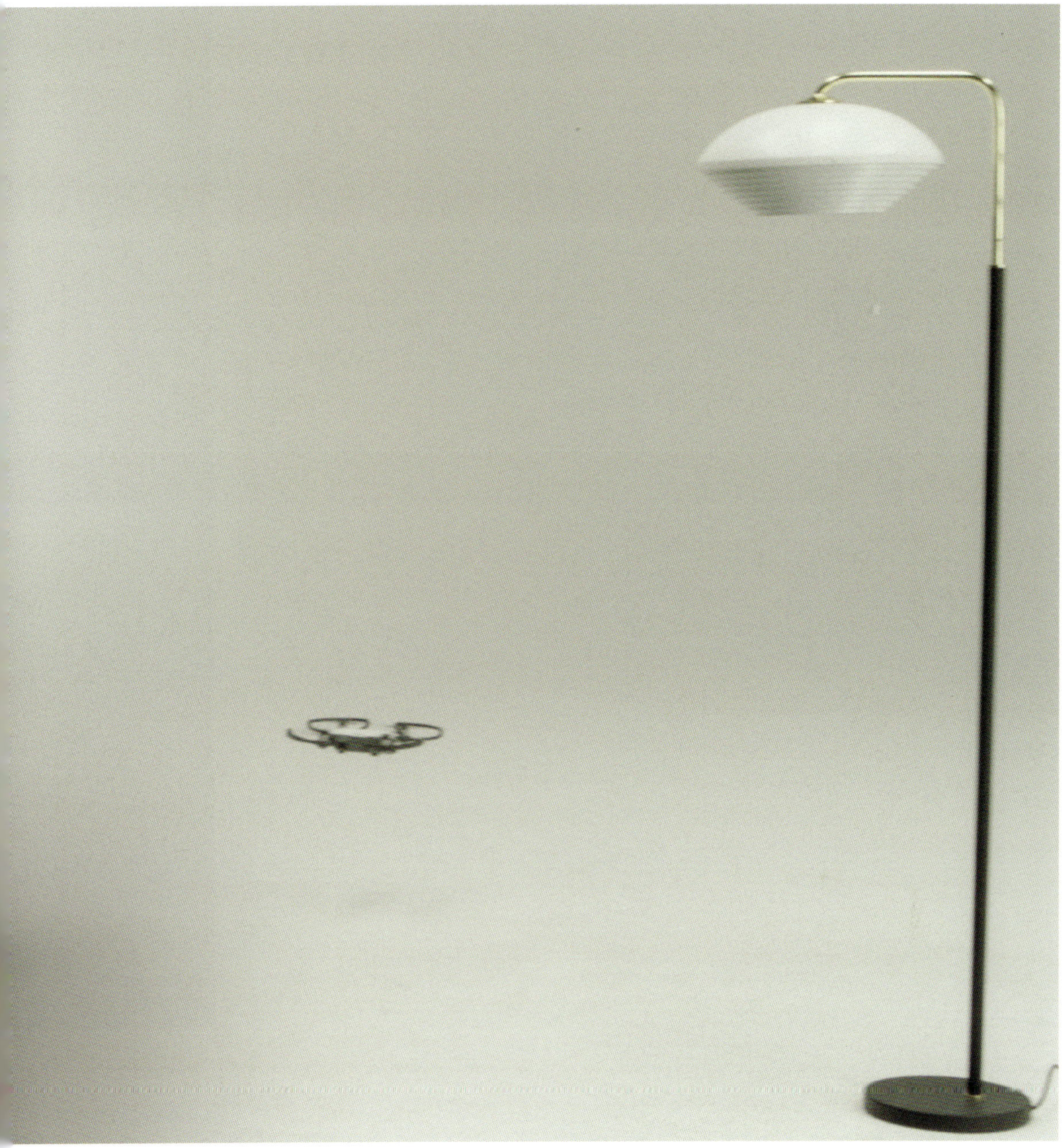

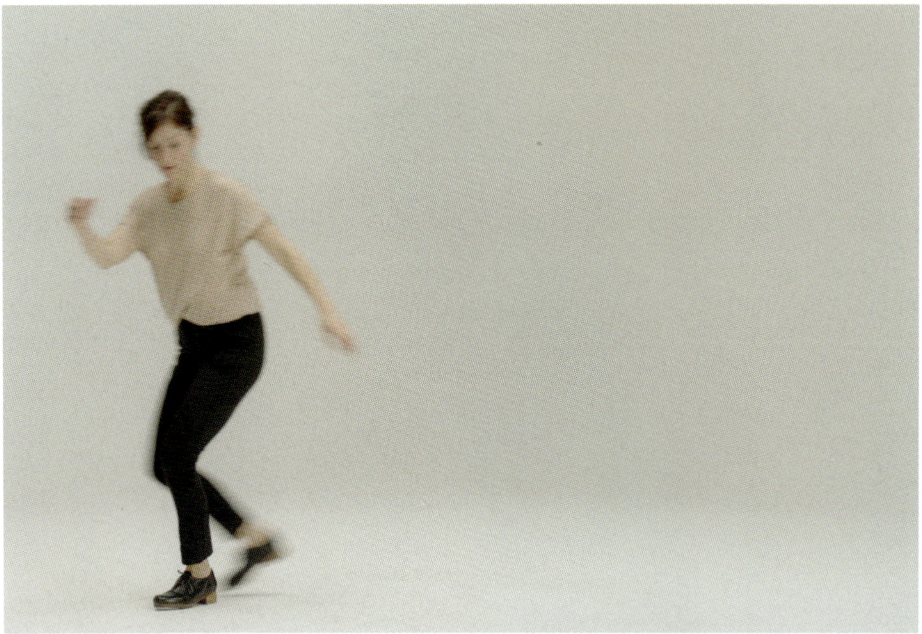

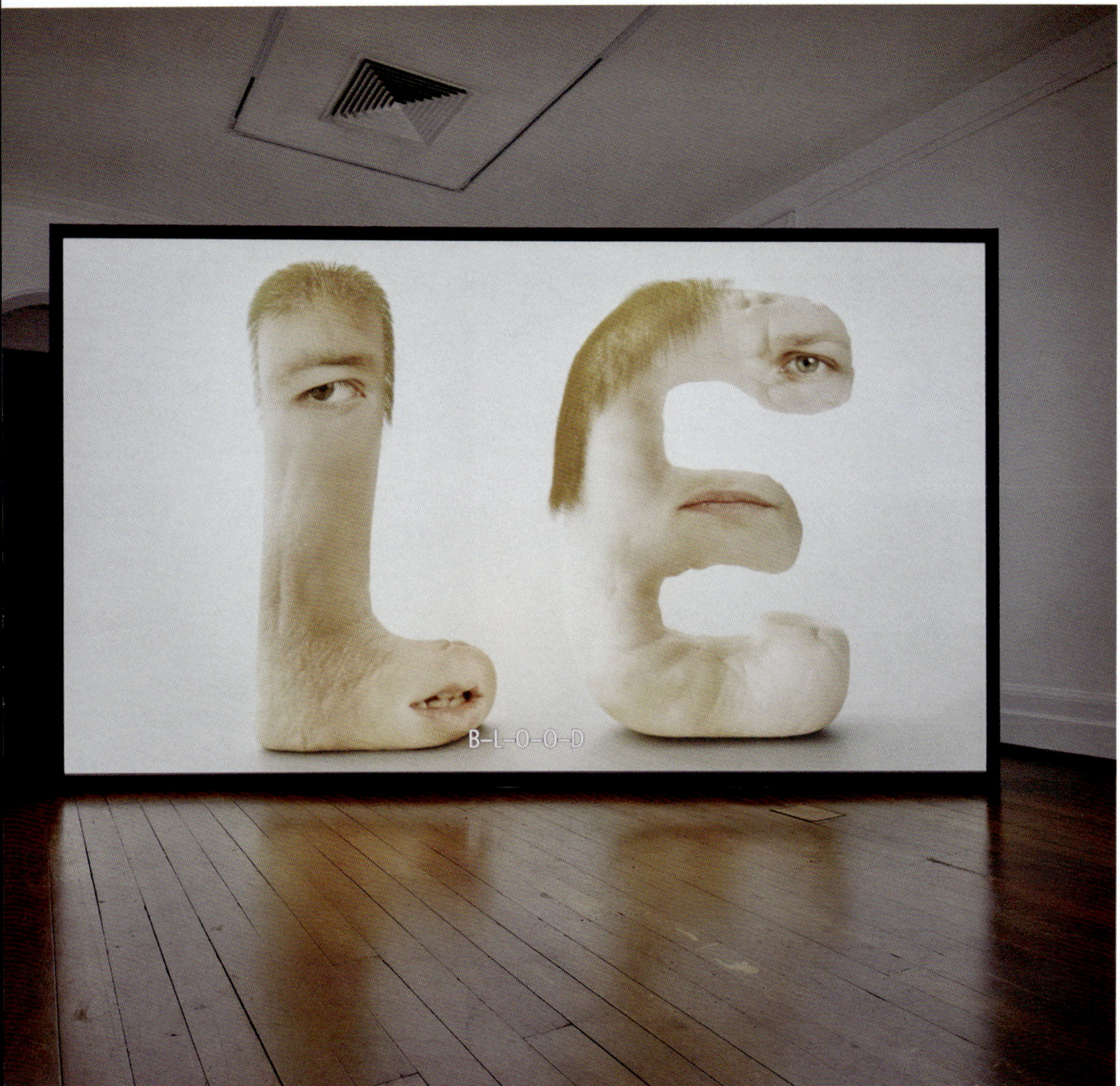
B–L–O–O–D

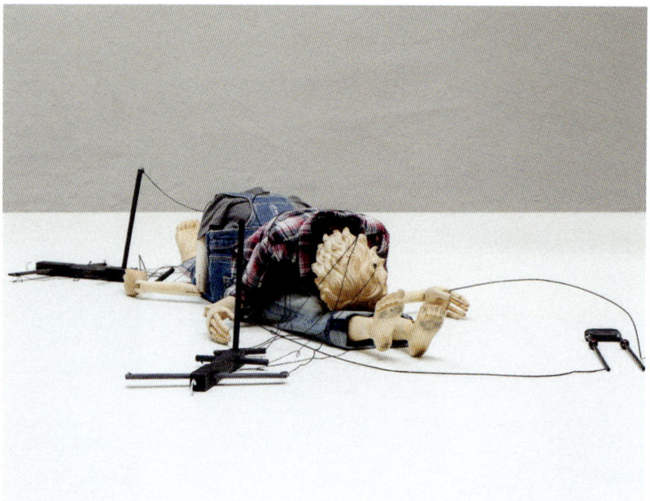

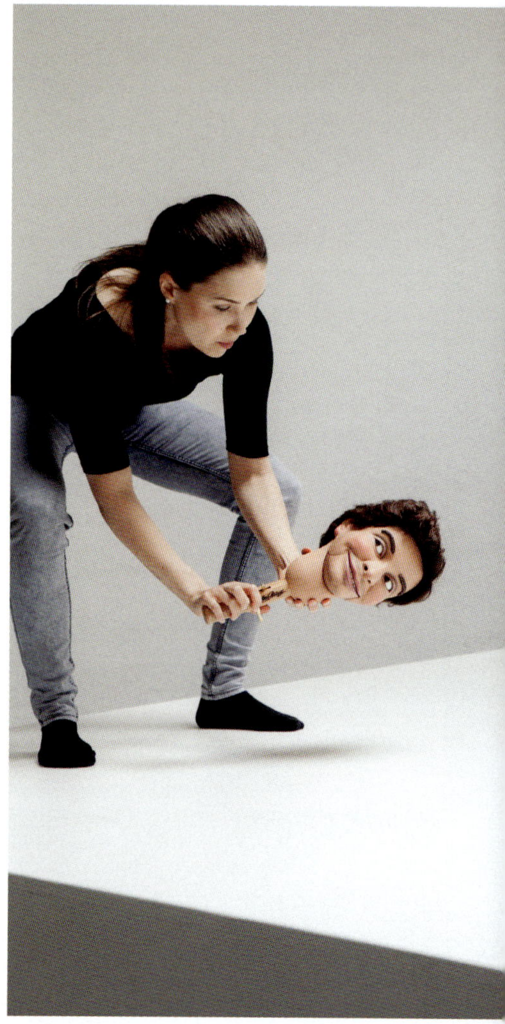

(19)

(20)

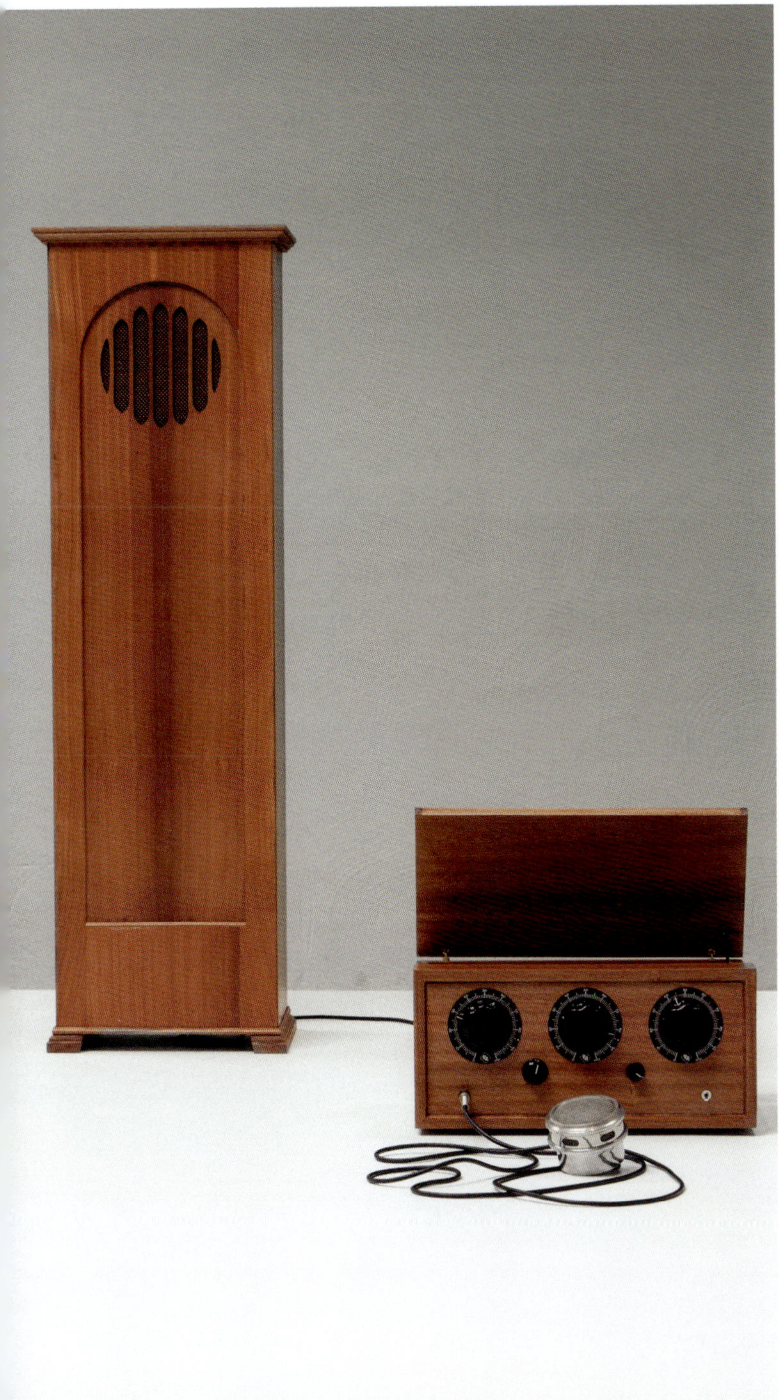

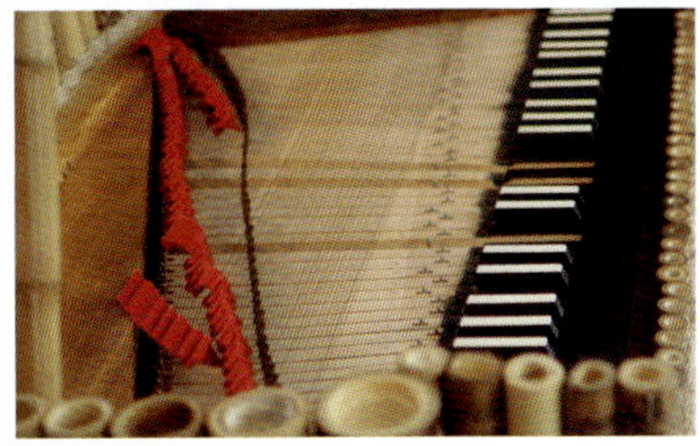

(21)

(22)

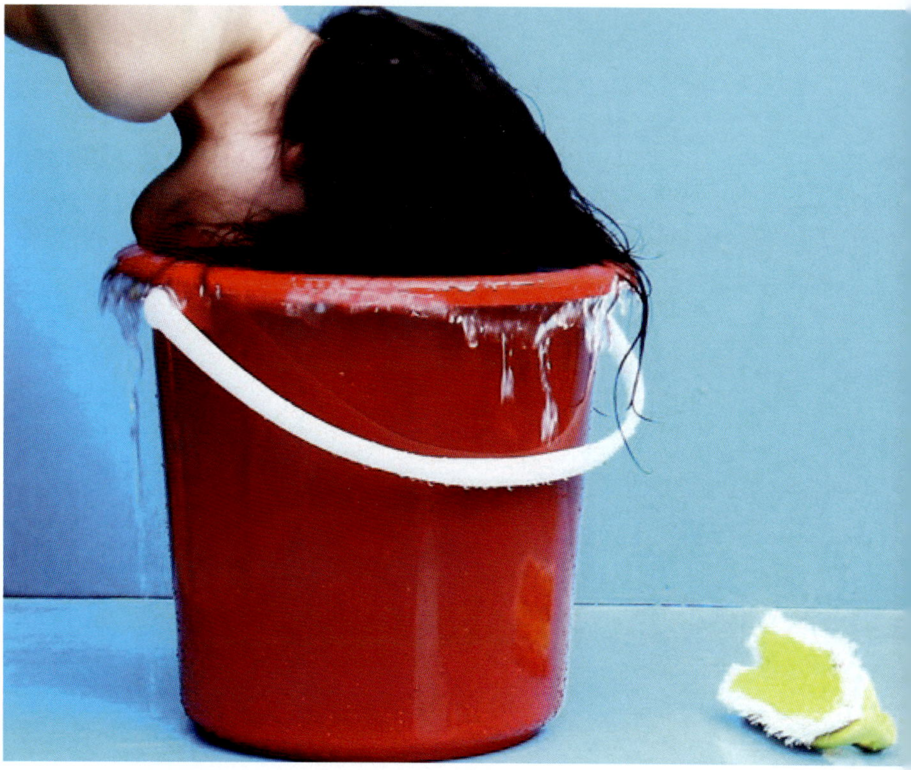

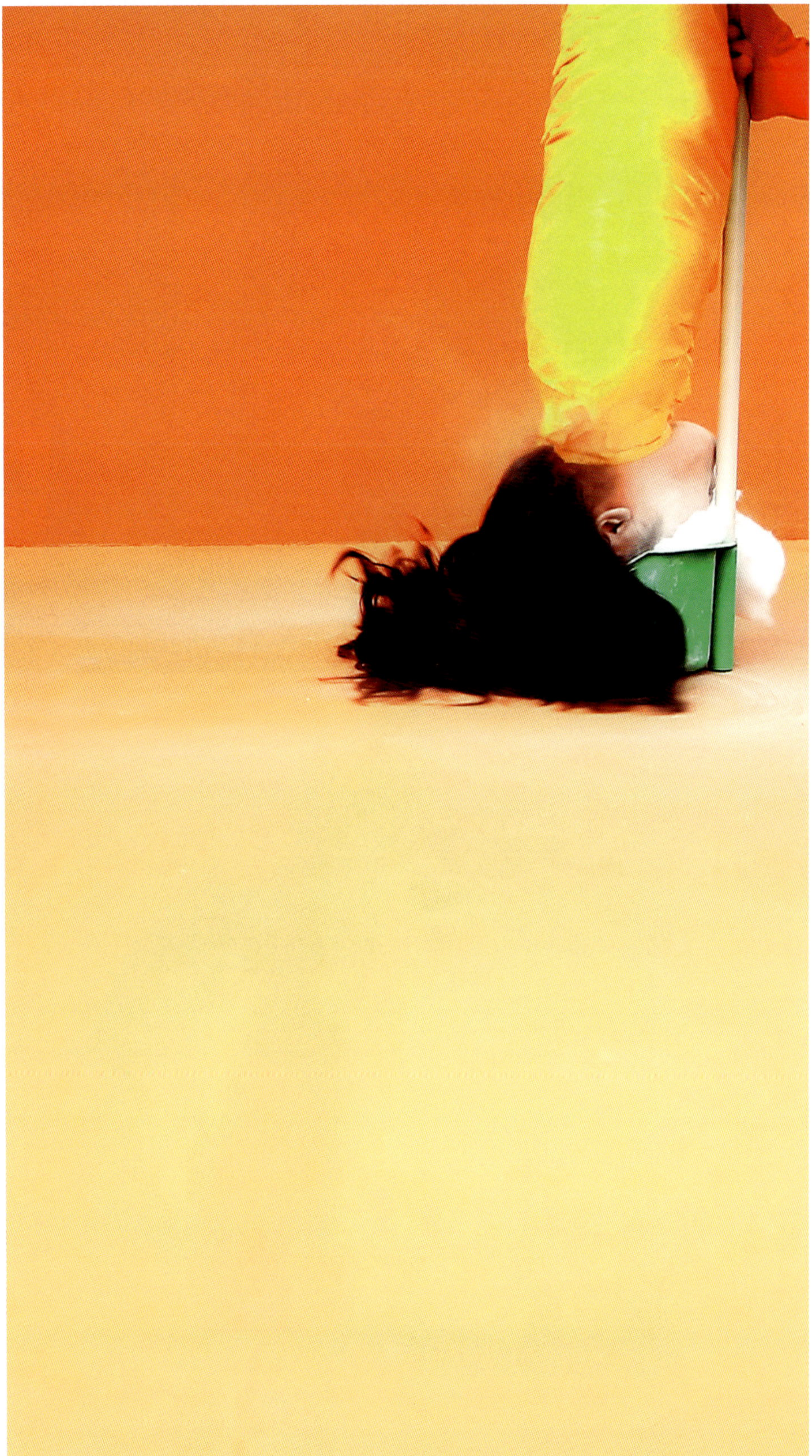

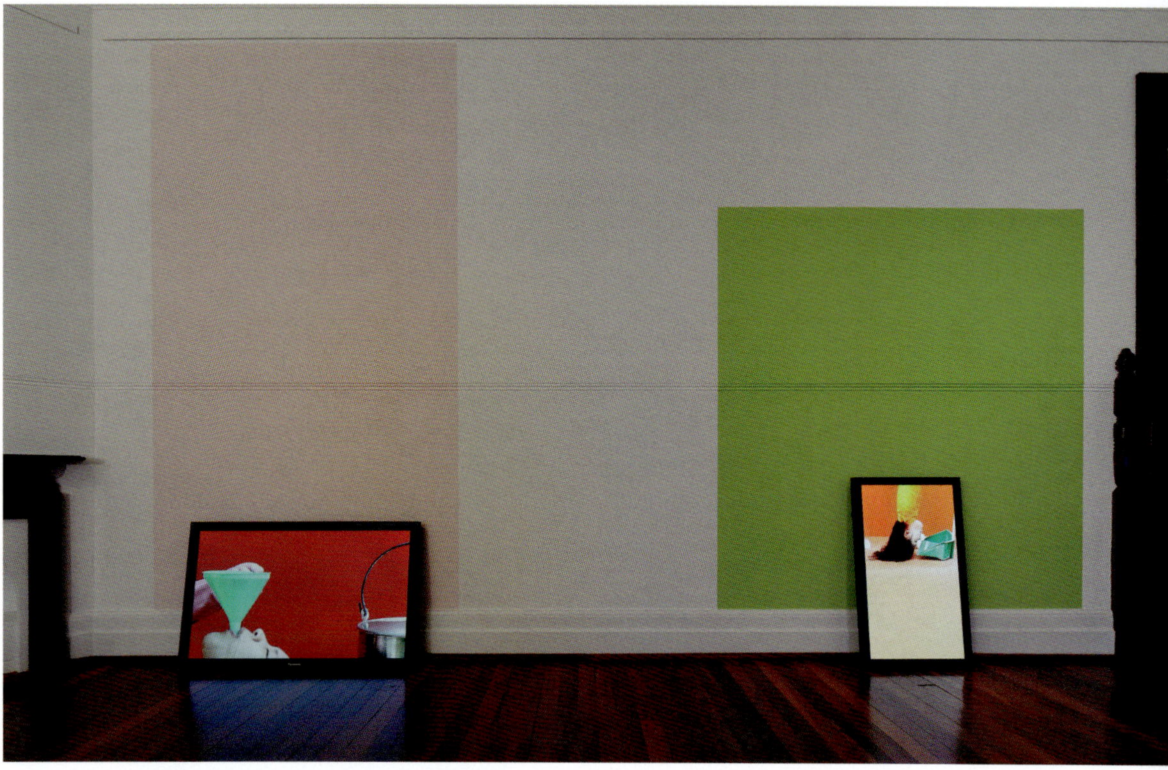

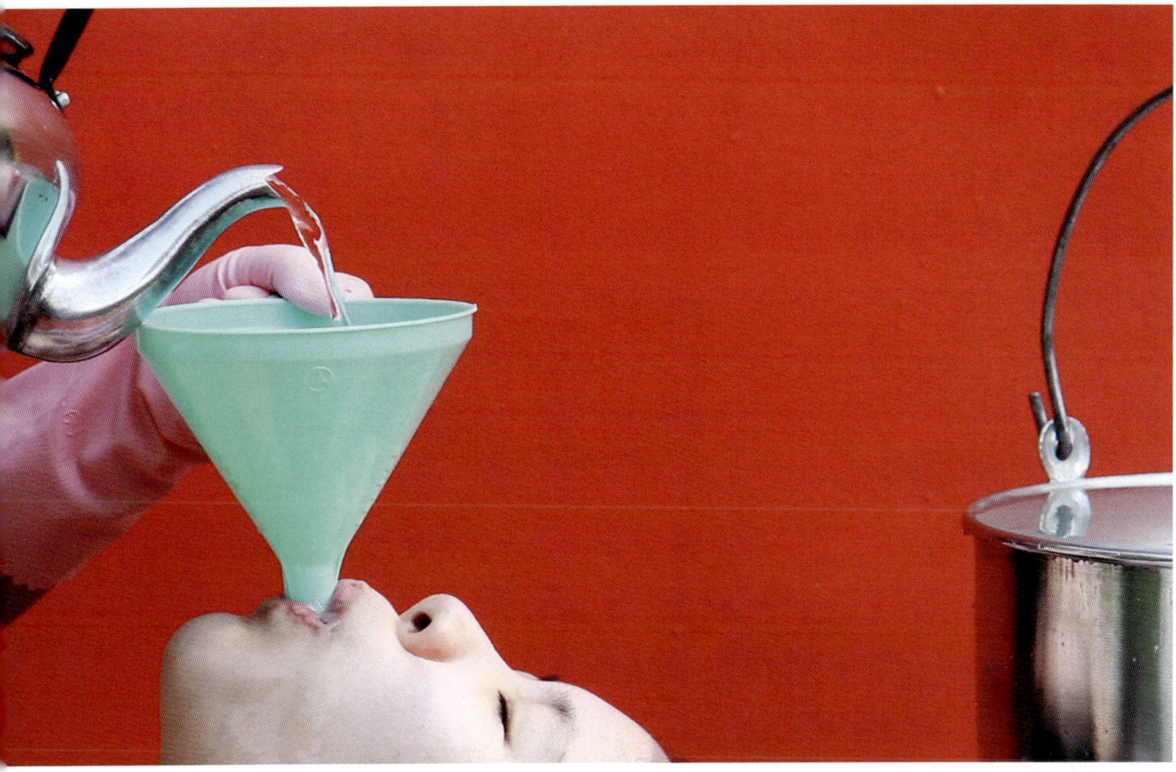

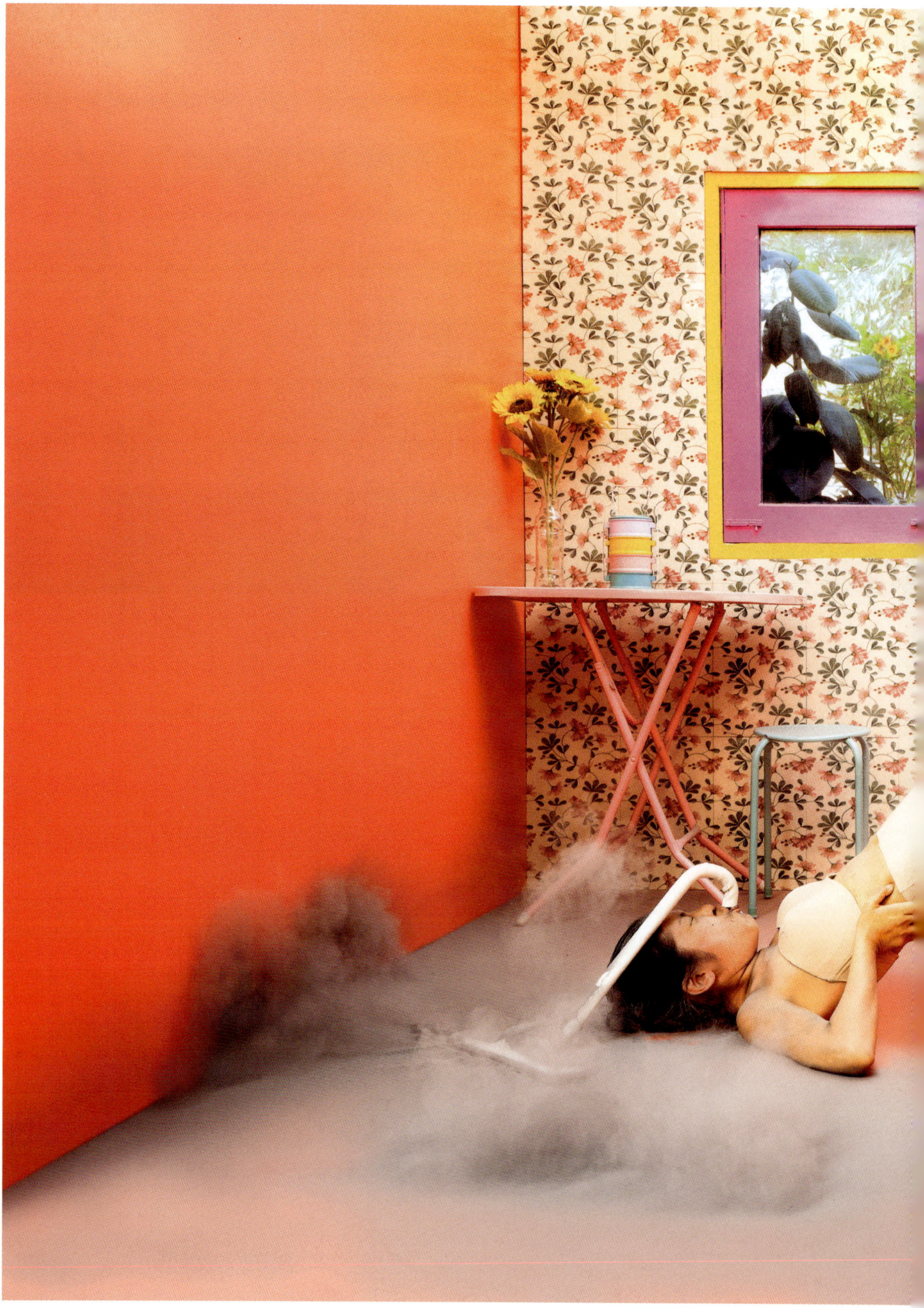

(27)

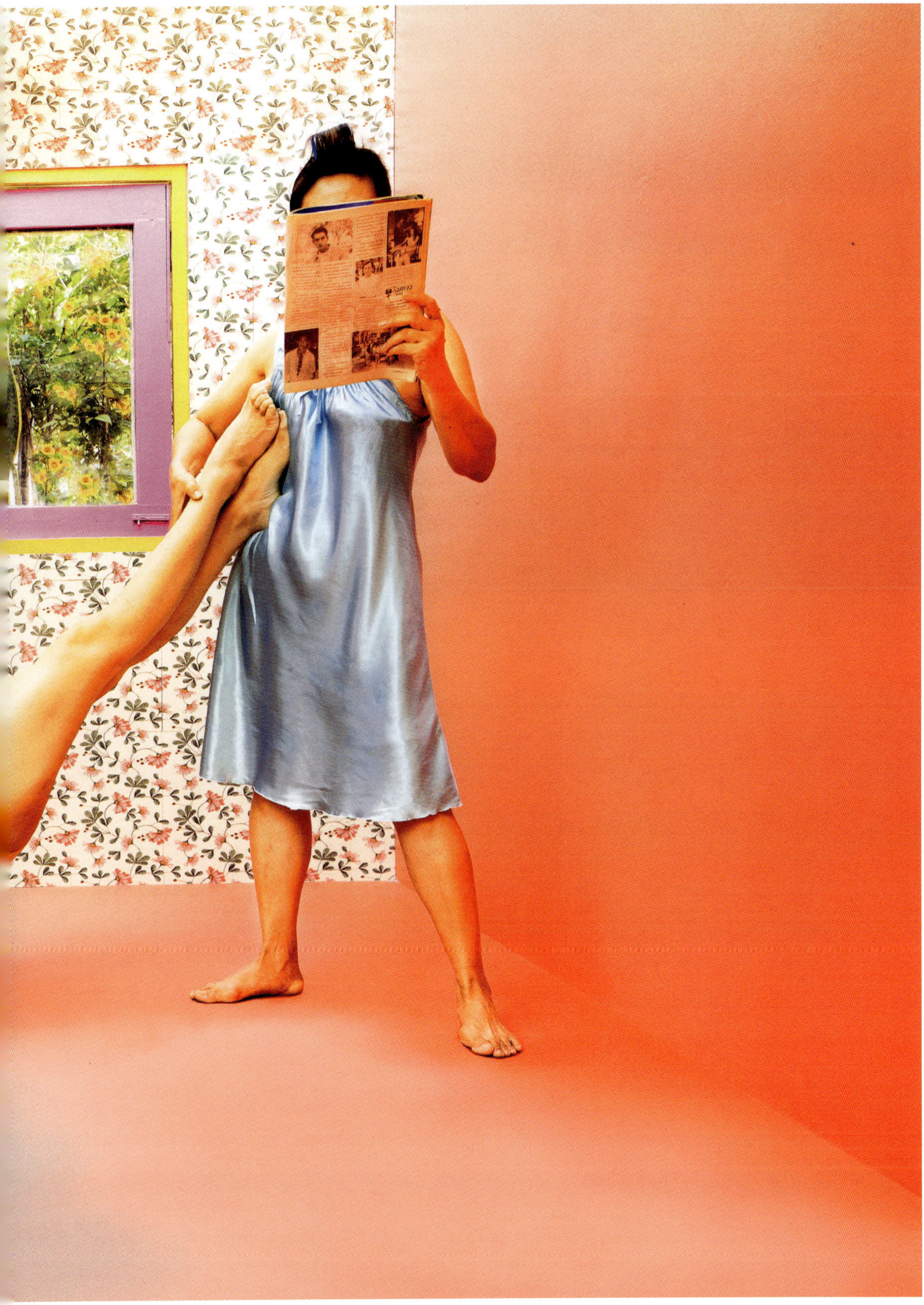

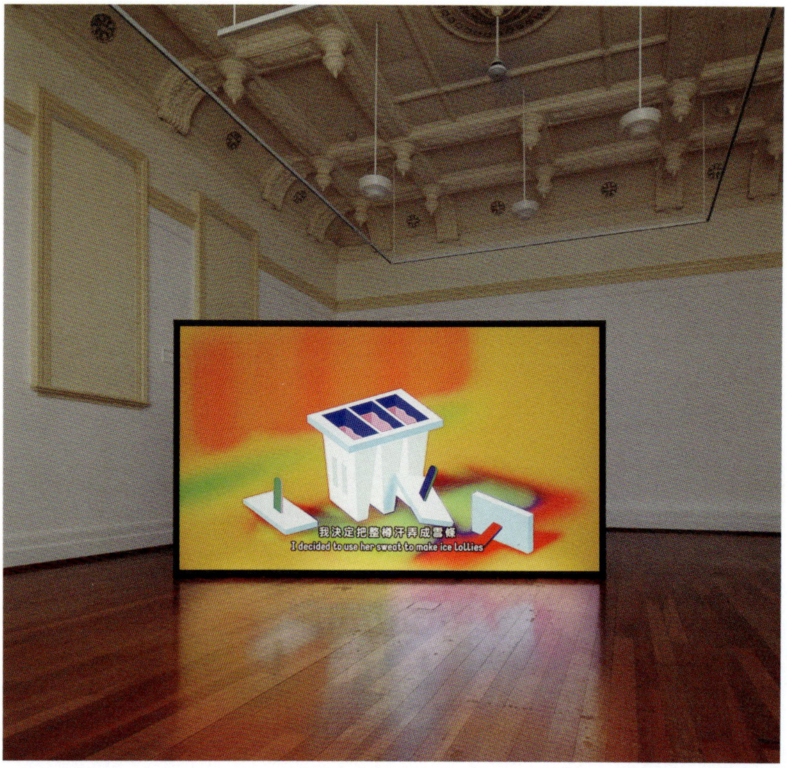
我決定把整樽汗弄成雪條
I decided to use her sweat to make ice Lollies

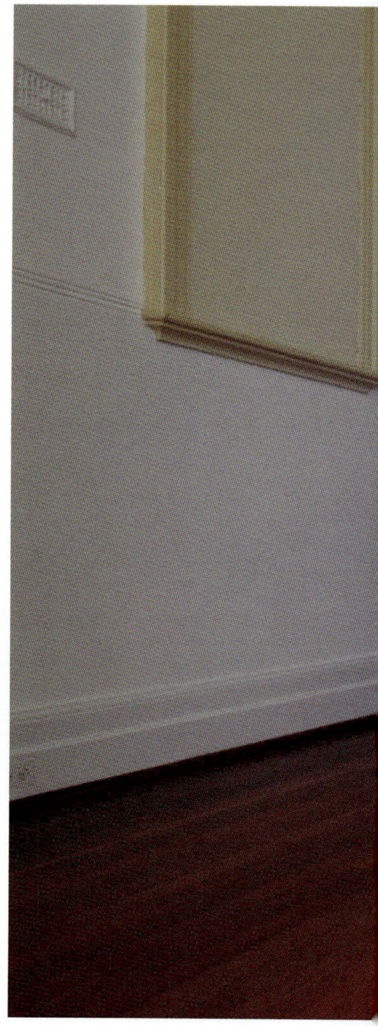

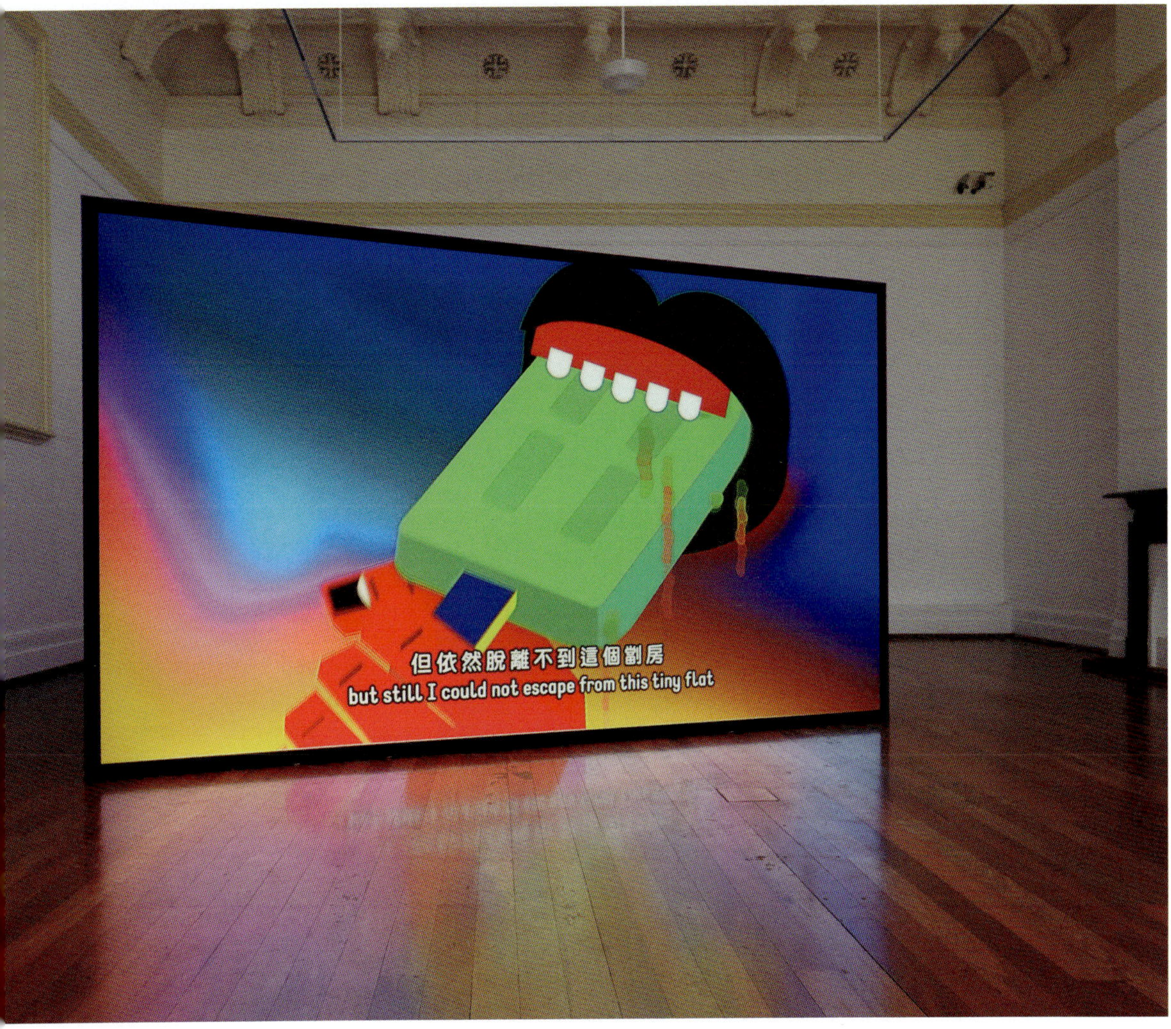
但依然脫離不到這個劏房
but still I could not escape from this tiny flat

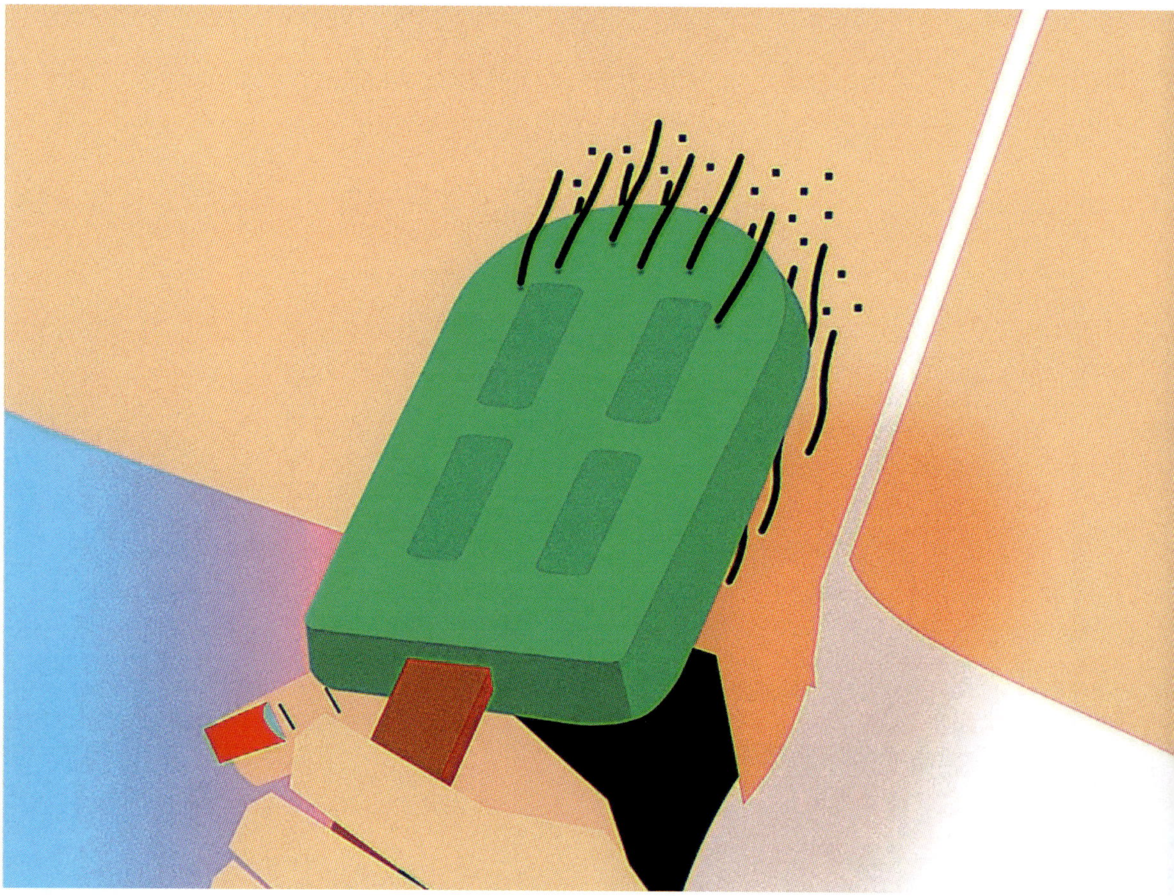

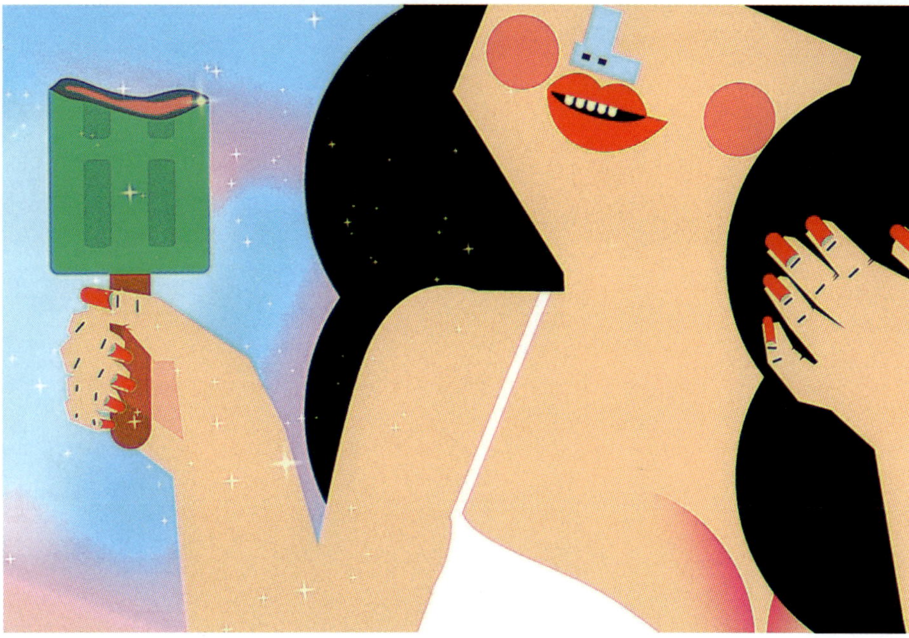

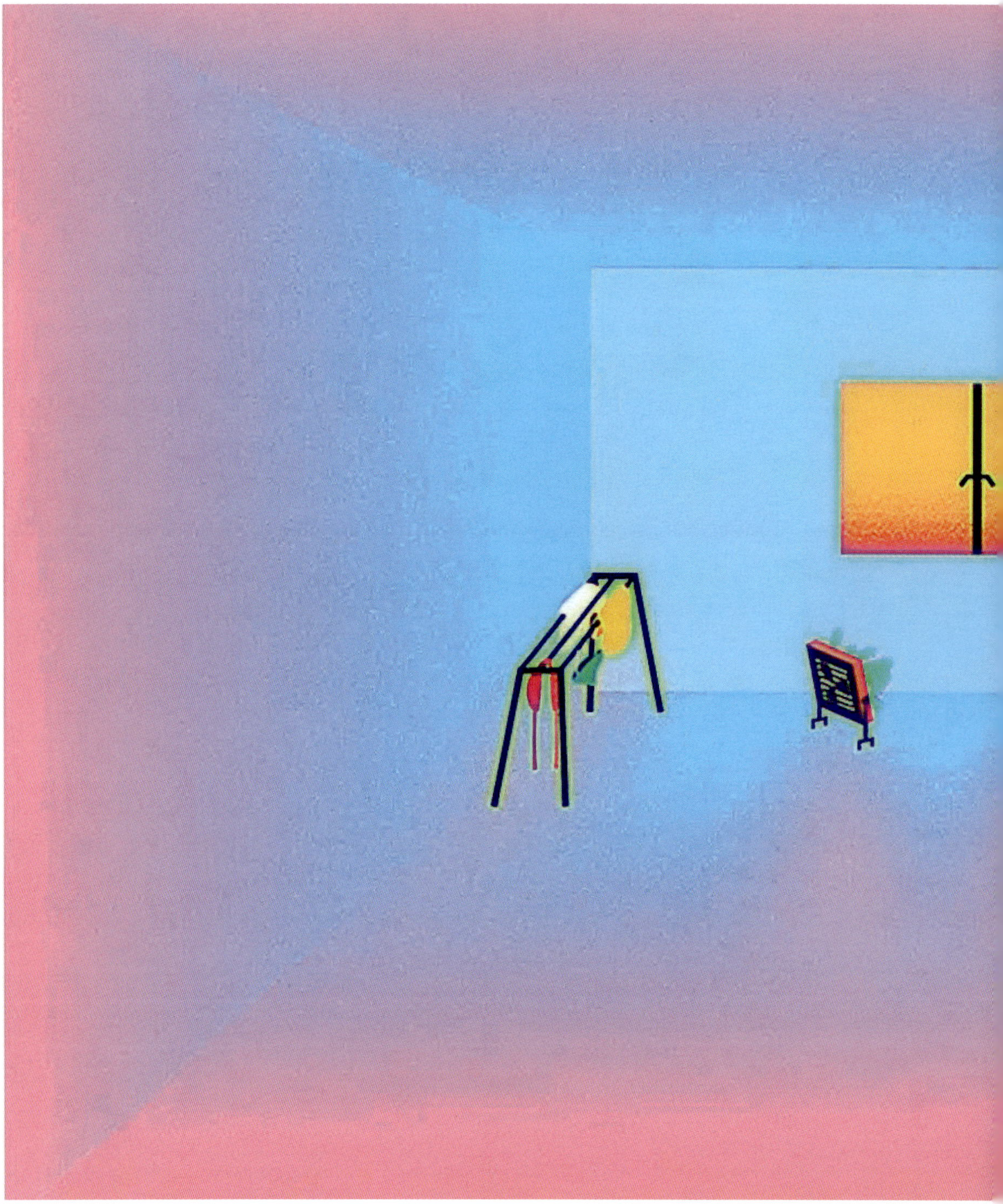

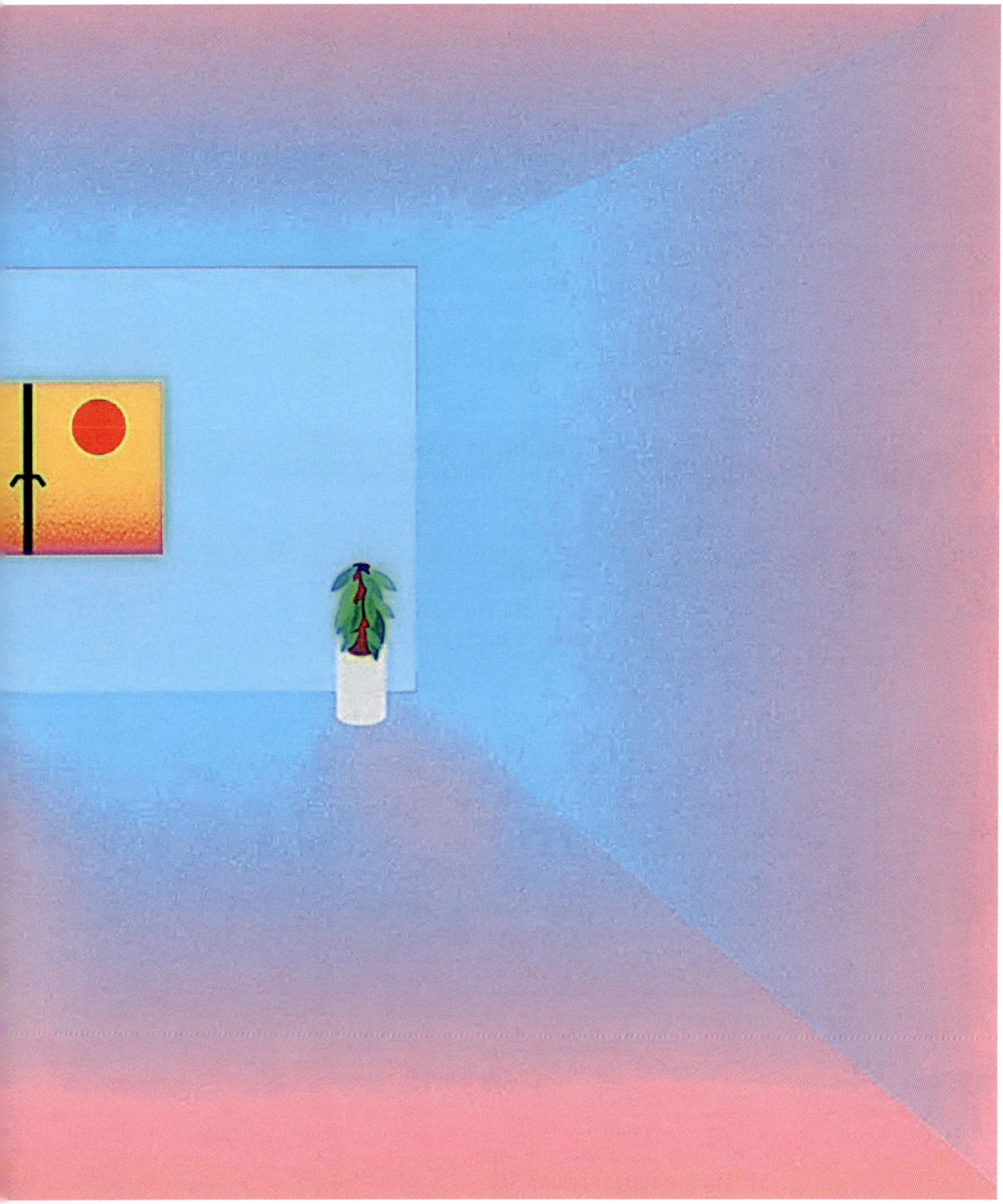

(01, 03, 04) Gordon Bennett, still from *Performance with Object for the Expiation of Guilt (Apple Premiere Mix)*, 1995, single-channel Standard Definition video, 4:3, colour, sound, 3 min 25 sec, looped.

(02) Gordon Bennett, installation view, BODIED, AGWA, Perth, 2020

(05, 08) Cheryl Donegan, still from *Head*, 1993, video with sound, 2 min 54 sec

(06) Cheryl Donegan, installation view, BODIED, AGWA, Perth, 2020

(07) Cheryl Donegan and Kawita Vatanajyankur, installation view, BODIED, AGWA, Perth, 2020

(09–15) Alin Huma and Cheiko Kawaguchil, *IOU*, 2003, digital photographic print, 30 × 21 cm

(16, 17) Jani Ruscica, still from *Human Flesh*, 2019, 2K video, stereo sound, 16 min

(18) Jani Ruscica, installation view, BODIED, AGWA, Perth, 2020

(19–22) Jani Ruscica, *Conversation in Pieces*, 2016, custom-made objects, live performers

(23) Kawita Vatanajyankur, still from *Soaked*, 2012, HD video, 3 min 31 sec

(24) Kawita Vatanajyankur, still from *The Dustpan*, 2014, HD video, 2 min 4 sec.

(25) Kawita Vatanajyankur, installation view, BODIED, AGWA, Perth, 2020

(26) Kawita Vatanajyankur, still from *Poured*, 2013, HD video, 4 min 43 sec

(27) Kawita Vatanajyankur, still from *My Mother and I (Vacuum III)*, 2021, 4K video, 6 min 30 sec

(28, 29) Wong Ping, installation view, BODIED, AGWA, Perth, 2020

(30–32) Wong Ping, video still from *Stop Peeping*, 2014, single-channel animation, 3 min 48 sec

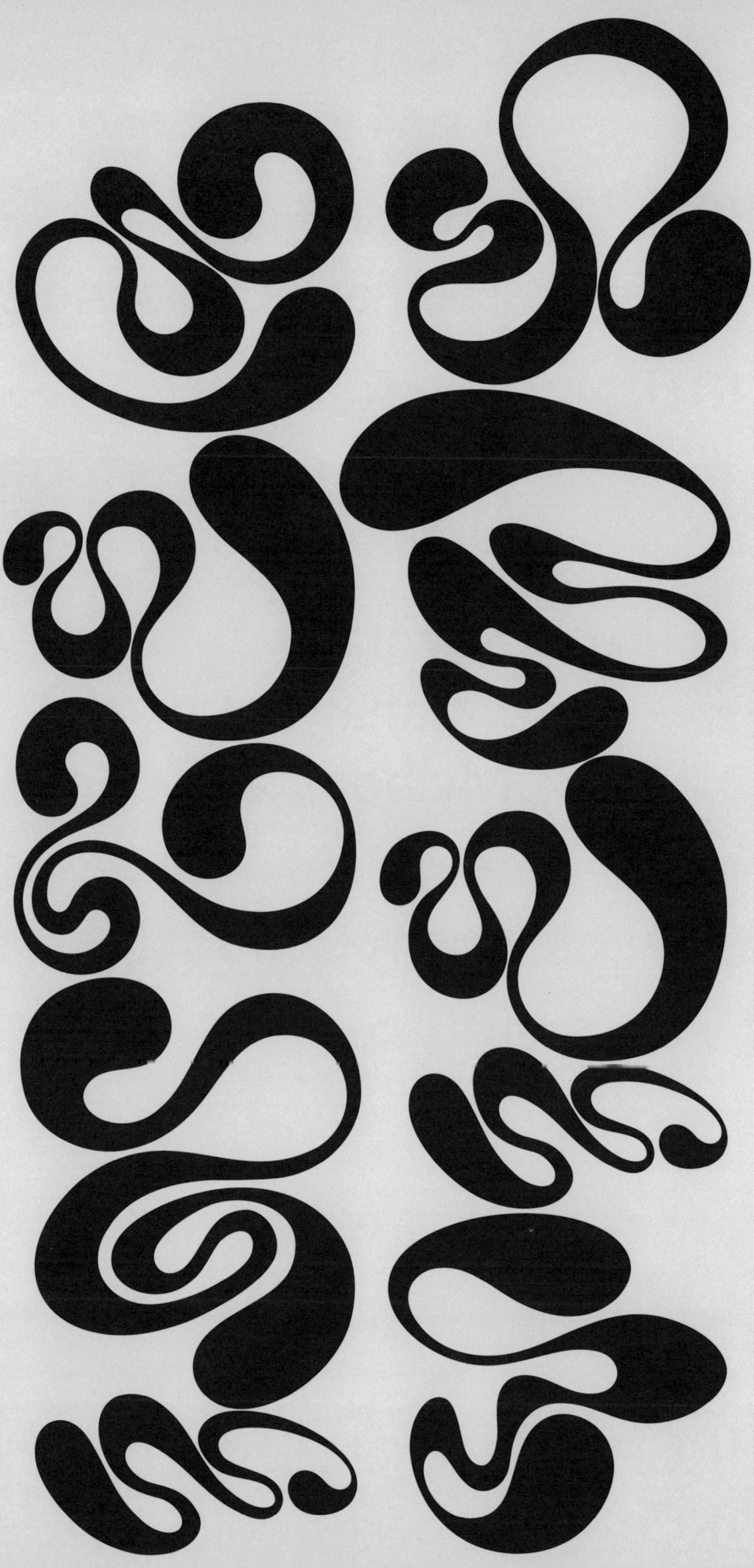

(01) Cheryl Donegan
It's all in the head

(02) Alin Huma
The hardest possible way

(03) Jani Ruscica
We become performative objects of language

(04) Kawita Vatanajyankur
My body as a domestic object

(05) Wong Ping
A happy accident

(RC) Rachel Ciesla
(RCo) Robert Cook

It's all in the head

This conversation took place via Zoom on 14 December 2020 between Cheryl Donegan in Massachusetts and Rachel Ciesla and Robert Cook in Boorloo/Perth.

RC Nine months into this pandemic we have all been experiencing a reconfigured sense of the physical body. This manifests in the different ways we hold the body, how we discipline and surveil the body, how we approach other bodies, and how we create divisions between ourselves and others. For us, your video *Head* [1993] was a way of addressing the moment while reaching back in history to see how people have always faced forces that shift us in particular ways.

CD It's interesting because it reminds me of the period in which *Head* was made in 1992 to '93. Around that time there was still the fallout of the AIDS crisis. I've been in New York since '84 and in the arts, but AIDS didn't really affect me or my lifestyle because I was straight and monogamous, and I wasn't exposed to drugs. So it didn't touch my life in that way, but still, it affected lots of friends and people I knew. And more generally all these topics were in the air: bodies, surveillance of bodies, spread, contagion, and sex. During the plague of AIDS all of that was definitely on my mind, and at the same time as all these aspects of pop culture. MTV was exposing bodies and viewing bodies. The way women's bodies were being looked at was changing because of people like Madonna. It all seems very long ago but it was a moment when we were facing lots of the things that you're talking about ... new technologies and new diseases.

RCo I was born in 1970 and so my awareness of AIDS was in 1983, my first year of high school. In Australia we had the infamous Grim Reaper ads with bowling balls: death would be bowling people over. As a child moving into adolescence, it felt like sex was instant death, no matter what. I grew up with that, and it feels very similar now with COVID – your proximity to other bodies, fear of sexuality, fear of closeness. Suddenly.

CD Yeah, exactly, and how it affects your youth lifestyle. Being born in '62, I'm in a different place generationally. When I was in high school, we got all the benefits of the sexual revolution. We could be in high school and get birth control pills at the clinic in town and not have to ask our parents or have them know anything about it. All this liberal wisdom from the '70s was still flowing and high school was quite wild in terms of people 'hooking up'. We didn't call it that then, but it was sex in cars and dark roads. We were just kids, but we were getting licence and permission from the culture to be a bit wild. Boy did that come clamping down for the generation later.

Of course you know, and I'm speaking generally, but in the late '7 high school kids in America were definitely closeted if they we gay. So I'm talking about heterosexual antics, but still we all got th freedom from the sexual revolution. Then AIDS came, and it real did change to 'sex equals death'. People younger than me and peop of different orientations were very affected by that. I think it definite contributed to my focus on fluids and, as we used to call it in gra school, the polymorphous perversities of sucking and spitting. Differe holes and orifices, all metamorphised by that laundry deterge container with multiple openings. It's phallic but it's also a breas I was in graduate school, I'd studied [Jacques] Lacan and all this w bubbling then ... boom!

It always shocks me how popular the work is. Even thoug it's quite old at this point, it keeps having relevance for people. But the time you'd see Madonna, William Wegman, Bruce Nauman, po music videos and video tapes of people doing things in the studio wit their bodies in different ways. I feel like I was at a crossroads and ju did what I did.

RCo It's fascinating that you mention Lacan and obviously there's also [Juli Kristeva on abjection, and [Luce] Irigaray on phallic containment and the feminin fluid. It's interesting then that you make this work that absolutely speaks to that pos structural feminist line of thinking but in a radically pop idiom. Was there a moment whe you were actually thinking about translating those theoretical ideas into something th would be viscerally felt rather than didactically worked through or explained?

CD Oh, absolutely. I don't know whether I was consciou that I would translate 'this as that', it was more that that's what I wa experiencing when I was an undergrad' and it was all just paintin painting, painting. Just get in the studio and move that materi around. That kind of thinking with your hands is a very good way t learn, though when I got to grad' school it was all in the 'head'. Sudden we were getting critical theory and being told that you need to hav an intellectual background to justify your work. It all just hit me like freight train. I felt so stupid and, even though it was very stimulatin intellectually, it also hit me emotionally because I felt so inadequat I realised, Oh, this is what it takes to be an artist too. I have to learn a this and read all this.

I think that I was struggling through all that, and questionin oil painting on canvas, because, even though you're making a big fat o painting in undergraduate school in 1983, some professor comes up an says, 'I can't tell a girl made that'. As a compliment! Literally stuff like th was happening and so you're like, 'right, I have to hide that I'm femal So, I used to sign all my work 'CA' so no one could tell my gender an they would take me more seriously. It's funny where you find yourse in terms of history. I really feel that I got the benefits as a teenager c free love but then the backlash of, 'well, there's never been any gre women painters'.

RCo It's funny that I didn't make that connection because *Head* is so overt sexual but also it's all in the 'head'. On one level the title is sexual but on another it' about being a cerebral artist as opposed to just painting things.

CD I think that's always been a personal struggle for me and maybe for a lot of artists. How can you be a cerebral artist and incorporate the criticality that you've learned about your position and culture *vis-a-vis* others, and still make work that is visceral, emotional, experimental? How do you put those two together? I think that for me it's a lifelong process of integrating those things.

In *Head* there's a whole other aspect to that denouement – where the spit of milk 'comes' on the wall and makes the stain. To me it was like action painting. It was, 'I'm here. I made my mark. I made my stain'. And it was connected to some notion of pleasure. The pleasure of, 'I made my mark'. I did my self-expression in the midst of this situation that I'd set up. It was almost like the situation had to occur in order for the expression to occur. For me, that truly was the takeaway for moving forward with how to make art. When I look back now at all the years of early video from '92 to 2000, and even beyond – because I did make video up until 2011 – a lot of it is, in a funny way, a primer for my thoughts, actions and self-expression as an artist. That period of work was about how to make things and what context to make them in. That's sort of the way I look at it now because I'm always trying to bring those two parts together, almost like the two parts of my education.

RCo So when you were putting yourself in the work, were you aware of the context of people like Bruce Nauman and Bob Flanagan and what they were doing in terms of being an artist/performer/subject?

CD I don't know if I was familiar with Bob Flanagan but Nauman and the idea of being an artist/performer was important. I think of his early work where he has ropes tied around his arms and calls it *Bound to Fail* [1966–67]. I mean, they're corny, but it's really playing with language in a Duchampian way. To me that's the pathway between the intellectualism of [Marcel] Duchamp and then, 'oh well, here's Nauman'. He's playing games with words, playing with the specificities and the vagueness of those terms, but he's also just stumbling around like Buster Keaton. He's playing a violin that he can't play but he's playing the notes on the scale for their literary content, D-E-A-D. Or he's bouncing a ball, like a little kid, and somehow proving something about space. So that just hit me as the place to be. And so, for a long time, I was like, well, how do you 'do' Bruce Nauman but address issues of painting or pleasure or feminism? How do you use his example but take on those issues?

RCo You mentioned MTV's commodification of women which became more and more prevalent through the music video medium. In relation to that context, did you try and elicit the particular responses that you got from the work? Quite famously, Collier Schorr's response captured the ambiguity of the work; how it could be read as both celebration and critique. Did you come to the work with a programmatic set of intentions or expectations about how it would be read politically?

CD I thought I did, but I was a little unprepared because to me I was calling it 'safe sex action painting' and 'stupid human tricks'. This related to David Letterman and how he would have people come out of the audience to show their stupid party tricks, like bobbing for apples or pie eating. Something disgusting that they have at a country

fair, where everyone's got their face in a pie and it's super sexual but n
one can say anything because it's the family fair. Letterman turned wh
was a corny '50s throwback into something sort of hip and ironic. S
I'm going to have all this milk flowing in my face and I'm going to t
to catch it in my mouth and spit it back. It's a bit of a 'hold my bee
action and so I thought it was funny. Then when everyone was comin
up to my husband saying, 'you really got something going on there br
I was fucking horrified. I'd have people, especially other women, saying t
me, 'has your dad seen this?'. Then it became, 'encore please, will you d
it with a keg?'. And then I was like, okay, clearly this has gone off the rai
Because if you haven't figured it out by now, I was raised Irish Catholic.
became super guilty. I was thinking I'd ruined my life with this. It was lik
a sex tape way before their time. But then I was thinking, what if sex tap
or porn are funny? I had to kind of live with it a bit. I always reckoned
was like having a hit pop song and then people want another pop son
that's just like it. But if you keep doing that you'll really ruin your caree
so you better move on and hope you can find the next thing.

RC Why did you choose the song by Sugar that you have playing in th background?

CD Maybe this piece lived so long because there were so man
threads to pull on. I remember at the time this movie came out calle
River's Edge [1986]. It was about a group of teens and there's a dea
girl by the river and it's like, who killed the girl? It was a really gre
angsty early teen movie that felt different because it was from a youn
person's point of view. And it was definitely pre-grunge, but it als
captured the grunge aesthetic because it was a youth culture movie an
it was very dark and very hopeless. These kids had nothing to do, it wa
the dead end of America, and it had a lot of beautiful themes. I won
spoil the movie, but the lyrics of the Sugar song 'A Good Idea' [199
were similarly about a dead girl by the river. And I don't want to kee
on pulling the thread for ever but there's a Bertolt Brecht poem abo
a dead girl by the river, and this sort of Ophelia feeling. So what do
that conjure? Youth and youthful tragedy, and not knowing what you'
doing so you just want to go lay down in the river. So in the song Bo
Mould keeps saying, 'it's a good idea, it's a good idea'. There was such
liquid theme about holding your head under the water and a sense
oblivion, almost like a sexualised oblivion, and it just felt okay. Yeah, it
a good idea. Bob Mould knows that I used it and he's never sued me
asked me for royalties. He was just like, you go!

RC That's good to hear. I've been kind of writing and feeling a lot of thing around that. About Ophelia in particular, about her drowning in the river because sh feels too much, and that tragedy is always political. I think female sexuality has long bee represented as akin to tragedy. So when you were talking about sex and death, I won dered about your prior work in the studio with the bread that is eaten by rats, and no being able to control your time, and how you were talking then about the female body

CD Oh, yeah, a hundred percent. This is definitely – no pu
intended – in the stream because the whole experience was me trying t
form myself as an artist and coming into consciousness. It was one thin

to try to mess about in the studio and make an oil painting to disguise myself as a man but was that really good enough? It wasn't going to get me anywhere, and so the painful part of graduate school and the period thereafter was tearing it all down and asking myself, What is my work? What should I be doing? Should I be baking cakes? Should I be making food art? Should I be just exploring? What should I be doing? Should I be sewing? In this really rudimentary sense I was breaking down materials and examining all of that. Then at a certain point I realised, oh no, it's all about language. Then, no, it's all about bodies. No, wait, is it language and bodies? And then you get a sense of how to use these things as materials. Maybe that's what I'm learning. What your materials might really be in a fuller sense.

The video that really precedes *Head* is *Gag* [1991], similarly indebted to Wegman and Nauman, where I had a loaf of French bread clasped in between my legs. It was coming up like a giant phallus, and I was sitting in a chair and I told the camera person, 'I'm going to lean down, I'm going to start to eat the bread, and I'm going to continue to eat the bread until I'm no longer flexible enough to bend over enough'. It was kind of like this auto-fellatio castration, and it was also physically difficult because I was eating a giant French baguette with no break, and no water. I'm literally hunched over and all you see in the video is the top of my head, and then I finally sit up, and it's like a sawn-off shotgun. It was me consuming this kind of phallic prosthetic, but it's only a loaf of bread. Like *Head* isn't really a breast or a dick. It's an entopic system with plastic bottles so it's going to end in exhaustion, with an 'I can't do this anymore'. But what was hopeful to me about that last stain in *Head* is that the two 'bodies' – me and that detergent jug – are trying to create a relationship of reciprocation and we can't because of this entropy. But the mark on the wall, that's not entropic. The mark is the result of all this. It's the thing that lasts.

Symbolically, when the action is played out, that's a way of getting out. So, is the stain on the wall the art? Whereas the act ultimately went away? I don't know, but I think all of that is like, question, question, question. It was just building this elaborate entropic machine with all these little parts in it: the music, the bright colours. It was made just to hang all that stuff on. I can say that now because it's been 30 years and I've talked about it a lot, but I think at the time that I made it, like in the song, I was thinking 'it's a good idea'.

RCo That's a brilliant interpretation in terms of bringing together the artwork as a critical vehicle and as an expressive vehicle. It seems to position your work quite uniquely in that regard, as you investigate the structures of language and power and being. And it also provides a way of not being contained by them and not (finally) giving over to the entropy. I wonder, therefore, how that idea has made its way out of the *Head* piece and beyond that point, through your practice. For instance, some of your other works, like *Cheryl* [2005], look at motivational discourses that transform people from one state to another.

CD I'm going to hold onto that description of an artwork being 'a critical vehicle and an expressive vehicle' because I think that's really important. That's everything isn't it? To have questioning, but the questioning doesn't just beat the poor thing into the ground so there's nothing left of it to be itself. The expression it gives you that can't ju be summed up. There's always an excess spirit. I think that – I hope tha – when a work *works* it can really have that quality. And I think it's funn that *Cheryl* couldn't be more different to *Head* – it represents a differe phase in which I was no longer in the videos. Maybe that was ultimate my criticism of *Head* – it shouldn't be about your body anymore, c about yourself in that way. Or if you are in the work, you have to be in in a different way.

So, I made this piece in 2009 that's called, *Stop Me If Yo Think You've Heard This One Before*. I talk in it, and I'd never spoke before. I repeat a monologue from an Andy Warhol film called *Nud Restaurant with Viva* [1967], and I'm trying to repeat the monologu through headphones as Viva speaks. It's a pretty weird video but als now that I think about it, it's ventriloquism. I'm transforming myself int the Warhol superstar while in the actual scene there's another Warhc superstar who's just listening. And so Viva is yammering and Taylc Mead is twiddling his thumbs and looking high. In my version, I pla Viva and my son, who was nine at the time, plays Taylor Mead. So it's completely weird dynamic because it's a parent and child … and I had set up on the monitor and I say to my son, 'just watch the monitor an do what he does, and I'm going to watch the monitor and say what sh says'. So we were watching TV and acting it out. But of course it wasn TV, it was this old bootleg movie.

It was about transforming and about motherhood. The ide of who the hell am I now? This is my studio in the apartment and I'v got two kids and I don't have a gallery. It was questioning, not just m identity, but the identity of space. Even the places I found myself – goin around with kids all the time, being with kids all the time; the places tha life takes you to. I think *Cheryl* came about after planning children birthday parties. Buying pinatas, just being in this world of taking car of all that stuff and just … perhaps finding out who you are in all thi So that's *Cheryl* … 'I have 1,000 customers'.

RCo Your work brings questions to emotions, and vice versa, in a kind c open emotionalism. Taking another step backwards in time, was that state of bein prevalent before you went to art school? And what pushed you to go to art school i the first place?

CD Yeah, it was definitely coming from that. I'm the oldes kid and so there's five behind me. Back in the day, parents weren't s hyper about kids' college and scores and grades, and it was sort of, wel you'll figure it out. Even so, I know my mom was disappointed becaus I got good grades in school and she thought that art school was nc for intelligent people. And she really didn't want me to go because sh thought it was a waste of, you know, brain power. Once I got ther I was like, Oh yes! This is where I need to be. Those years were amazin years. Of course I was miserable, with a cigarette pack rolled up on m sleeve and torn t-shirts and the whole punk rock thing, but we wer encouraged to just work in the studio like professional artists. Just work work, work, and it was really good because I really learned what it' like to be in a studio and make art. It was definitely the place for me I was glad I went.

RCo Maybe as a way of wrapping up ... a lot of what we've been discussing has been about setting ideas in action but also about methodologies of practice. Could you talk a little about your approach to the methodology? How you think about the idea and its action – but also its evolution – through your work. Amateurism is important and within that a kind of experimental mindset. Some of the install shots of your exhibition *My Plastic Bag* [2017, Kunsthalle Zürich] seem to indicate a laying out of a problem without necessarily having a specific resolution to it, and yet obviously it encapsulates something formally.

CD Well, I'm glad you see that. Simply put, I've tried to learn to not talk myself out of ideas. I think there's a tendency – well, everybody does it I suppose – to talk yourself out of ideas because everything does seem kind of stupid until you do it. It's almost as if you've got to see it in the room, make it manifest, to really know if it's good or not. Because sometimes when things manifest, they're not as stupid as you thought they were – they actually have their own properties that you almost can't imagine. You just have to start your ideas, see what they look like, see what else they say, and then adjust from there. I think seeing what it is and actually dealing with the idea – instead of just keeping it all up here and having a fight with it exclusively abstractly – is an important thing that I learned.

This is harder to do now though, with the art market. The way it's codified for its own convenience around, literally, what the lifecycle is supposed to look like for an artist. The older I get the more horrified I am by that. So many people are so constrained because of the demands to fit what this thing needs – its convenience, its schedule, its strictures. How did it get like that? We could probably trace it for a while, but the older I get the more I think it's crazy because it doesn't allow for the kinds of things that could be fruitful. Of course, I still think finish and mastery of materials are important. Knowing what materials can do and not being afraid of them. Learning to make them do what you want. But experimentation and mastery go hand in glove don't they?

RC Weirdly, as curators, it's nice to hear that. That sense of just testing something out, seeing what happens. There's a way of making exhibitions around that idea too.

[01] Cheryl Donegan

Cheryl Donegan's *Head*, 1994, is one of the best-known works in video art. The work resulted from a situation in which the artist tried to swallow milk from a laundry container. In DIY spirit she performed *Head* to a backing track played from a boom box in her studio, relying on no post-performance editing. The video was a punkish counterpunch to the representation of women in MTV videos at the time, simultaneously celebrating assertive female sexuality and critiquing its commodification. In *Head* Donegan becomes the medium, acting out what is possible within the constraints of the situation.

Cheryl Donegan was born in 1962 in New Haven, United States of America, and works in New York. Her first career survey *My Plastic Bag* was held at the Kunsthalle Zurich in 2017. Other major solo exhibitions include GRLZ + VEILS organised by the Contemporary Arts Museum Houston and Aspen Art Museum in 2018. Donegan's work has been included in the Whitney Biennial of American Art, New York (1995); Venice Biennale (1993); Biennale d'Art Contemporain de Lyon (1995); and the Semaine Internationale de la Video in Geneva (1997).

The hardest possible way

This conversation took place via Zoom on 16 December 2021 between Alin Huma in Tokyo and Rachel Ciesla and Robert Cook in Boorloo/Perth.

RC So whereabouts are you? Are you in Tokyo at the moment?

AH Yeah, I mean I might as well be on Mars. I'm in a great space right in the middle of Shinjuku...

RC This show [BODIED] happened a year ago in December 2020. At the time we were still in the midst of a pandemic and there was a heightened sensitivity around the body and its parameters, and how it was being made visible.

RC It was almost as if there were 'scare quotes' around everyone. We wanted to put a show together that wasn't about those larger social issues but that made you aware of this 'square quoting'. Your work [*IOU*, 2003] made with Cheiko, fitted beautifully with that premise. The performativity of the work; it's lo-fi nature; it's sense of reclaiming something on the verges of experience – or indeed the world – as we were all being sliced off from things. In the room containing your work we also showed a Gordon Bennett video that is super punchy and also about language in its disciplinary function. So your work sat as a material echo of that.

Could you begin by talking about how you made that sequence of images and some of the decisions around its material form as a publication?

AH To put it really simply, that body of work was basically just what I was doing at the time. I was with Cheiko doing this and that. And she was not actually an artist at all, and even 17 years later, she's still not an artist. I'm probably saying more than I mean to; I'm coming from a point that has actually affected my own art practice, and still does. My art practice has always been surfing pretty close to the real, and I always find the real more interesting than making art. Part of me has always resisted making art. I still do, and for quite some time I really wanted to make movies. Every time I go too far in one direction, I'm like, wait a bit, it's better to be the person in the movie: to let life sing. But I make art because I have always had some kind of hook or some kind of understanding of what that art thing is. Art is a bourgeoise thing after all. I come from communism, and my parents were the intellectual class, the third class. What was it – the hammer, the sickle and the brush?

So my art practice was basically what I was doing at that time – and I was supposed to have an exhibition at AGWA and so I showed a bunch of things and this book was one of them. Which was a bit shit; I basically applied all the stuff they teach you at university. I was trying to do the 'right thing' because that's where I was at the time. I ha a good artist-friend and he was making art with non-artists, but he wa doing it 'officially' with the institution's approval. Whereas for me it wa like a 'dirty secret' that I was sneaking the non-artist into the museum.

So, for that show I asked Cheiko to co-author the boo with me and she agreed, without quite understanding what tha actually meant – something I only realised much later and not withou consequences and complications. As far as taking photos is concerned, generally feel that the other person – the subject – does more than hal the work and that felt particularly true with that piece. So the whol process was very close to crunching through the real.

RC Is there something in there about making things harder for yourself Maybe it's too 'easy' to make work, call yourself 'an artist', do the art things, run th methodology out.

AH I don't know if I really mean this, but there's somethin to doing things in the hardest possible way – and maybe that's wha art is for me. I don't mean doing it in a stupid way, more like goin down to that molecular level. I'm doing that in almost every aspec of my life as well as art making. It's not really worth it otherwise. So guess I'm just doing things in a way that has integrity by my standards They're very self-defeating and self-sabotaging ideas. And, of course the fact that I'm doing most of this outside the gallery system doe get a bit annoying. But then again, as far as that goes, like [Franz Kafka says, 'It's like this big …' Sorry, I think I'm going off into th misunderstood suffering-artist motif. Whatever the case, the 'artist a such' – including Kafka and [Vincent] Van Gogh – always had peers friends, family. There was always some select group, however small of people who were just enough. Enough that they were not just tha pathetic struggling artist. I don't believe in that cliché whatsoever, bu I do sound like some nineteenth-century artist. That's not what it' about these days.

RC So there's just enough people to keep you going – like a sense of a audience, someone who gets it – and that's enough to sustain you. You seem t have reached across borders and margins of various types, into fashion and als literature to a degree. And your practice kind of shuffles across various notion around art/non-art and mediated life. Is that because you are trying to keep, or t find, different types of relationships with people? Is it to slot your practice into th margins of something?

AH Yeah, I evoked the nineteenth-century artist but maybe it' more like the Chinese literati, or the Renaissance when they were doin everything: art, music, food, politics. It's all really important. But image are going in a different direction; it sounds silly but there are too man of them. I think that is where things are at right now. And maybe it' kind of absurd to be into fashion too. But I'm still excited about thi time as opposed to even 10 or 15 years ago. I don't think it really make sense to be into either photography or fashion – specifically into one a opposed to the other. I'm not going to just be the stupid fashion guy, o the artist guy. Of course there is that other bullshit level where you hav to be different and you (eventually) become a caricature of yourself. This is what you need to do to have a career in anything. You have to be a real genius not to do it, but very few people can avoid it. So that's part of the reason that I'm into fashion but not quite in it. It's the same with 'photography'. I can't get any professional work doing photography, but I know enough photographers who really respect what I do and get what I do. It's helpful that I've been this way for my entire life, and I'm basically how everybody is now. You have to be a good photographer these days. Everybody has to be. You have to be a good anything. Lately I've been thinking more about economics and practical things. Because you have to be good at those too. And maybe those are the things I've neglected a little bit.

RCo In hindsight maybe it was a bit weird for us to just pick fashion to talk about because there are many things to connect to in your work; for example you were doing the coffee thing, the vintage bikes. Has there always been a broader idea about 'the aesthetic' at work for you?

AH To me it's all about making a *space* where things can happen. So a book is a space. That magazine I was doing is a space. When you ride a bicycle you make a space.

RCo I guess you could look at it like there's a space for aesthetics and then there's a space for a kind of pragmatism. Is there a tactical dimension to that for you, in terms of things you need to do to get other things to happen?

AH Oh for sure. It's like cooking, where you are following a recipe and there are a million factors involved. But, as I said earlier, I've been a bit low on the practical and economic side ... tactically speaking ... [laughs].

RCo And then where is the philosophical dimension. How are you deciding: why this and not that? What are the choices that operate those parameters?

AH I think that those choices always make themselves. They're obvious – and this is kind of my point – if you've made that space, and if you see things for the units that they are, then the choice just makes itself. I know it sounds dull but it is like in the Zhuangzi: the man who is chopping the beef, who never has to sharpen his knife in 18 years because if you touch it in just the right place, the carcass just undoes itself. That's very much like how decisions get made – you just sit back and make the space, or just look at the space. So in a way that's what that book you're holding [*IOU*] is about. It's about a person, Cheiko, who has a strong presence and I'm there with the camera. I was quite annoyed at that time, especially in Perth, because people were like: oh, it's performance photography. I preferred the Sydney response. The Sydney scene was all about *Purple* magazine at that time and *Doingbird* had also just started. The 'image' as opposed to the 'performance' seemed to be more elegant and more what I was trying to do. It had been too much struggle before. And – how should I put it? – maybe I do enough struggle in real life. I'm happier if the image can just exist. My friend, Pierre Toussaint is one of the world's slickest photographers and he thinks my photography is really glossy and polished. I know my photos look the opposite, but they're no People like Pierre can see that; they know what I'm trying to say.

RC I have a friend in Melbourne who's a designer. A while back I wa wanting to make a 'zine and he said, 'I've seen a really good one by this guy wh was in Melbourne for a little while. I feel like they were printed on Bible paper. H probably printed them in Indonesia. And I can't remember his name but maybe h was Romanian'. And then I moved to Perth, did this show and I was like, 'Oh my Goc that's the same person!' My friend was talking about your *F de C Reader* [2012–13 and he said it was really slick.

AH Yeah, a lot of people saw it as offensively shabby, so I'r happy to hear that. That's just reconfirming something I knew in th first place – that it would have a cut-through. There have probably bee 500 people, who I know of, who thought that was the best magazin they have ever seen.

RC You went to Indonesia to do these? And I heard that you did thousand of them, is that right?

AH Have you seen the third one? Oh you've got it! Oh my Goc That is the funniest thing ever! Making that nearly killed me. It's th stupidest thing I've ever done, but I think it's the best thing I've eve done to actually wrap it all together between two covers and finish i Also, there are probably 200 endurance art projects embedded in it tha went nowhere. I think they're all crap. None of them went anywher near a pilot, a mock-up. Some of the writing and a lot of other thing in it are great, but I don't think there is any great content as such. Bu the logic and the way it came together, I think that's great. So, if I coul do that with good content, more time and good people, it would be freaking great magazine! You wouldn't be doing that magazine now bu at the time it would have been great. But it never really got to that poin – maybe it's more like a proof of concept.

RCo What's interesting is that you talked before about the importance o a few people being around you, or the 500 people who've seen this magazine, bu for the 'reader' it is a mass or bulk thing. The magazine was an object to be carrie around, you could put it in your back pocket and carry it with you on your bod And so in my mind there's an idea of it being like a mass of people.

AH A mass of people. But what do you mean?

RCo Well, if you make many thousands of something, there are man thousands of people that may or may not have these items on them. It's quite, hmn ambitious is the wrong word, but it's a big gesture to make a lot of something and t get it out into the world.

AH Maybe it has something to do with the fact that the firs show I ever had was in a museum. I had been making work for 1 years, actually longer, yet never thought I should have an exhibition i some small, sceney space as one usually does. Then all of a sudden I'r confronted with the thought that potentially a million people are goin to see the work. It's sobering in a particular way.

Then there's the other side of the 'mass' thing. I actually sat down once, a long time ago, and analysed this. I realised that for me to see something I do as 'art', it had to separately click on precisely eight different levels. And for a collective piece, like the magazine, it would be eight to some power (maybe the number of other contributors). Anyway, for it to work, what I need is some density. Which is funny because I see myself as a minimalist, I sure like simple things. I guess you have to earn your minimalism the hardest possible way, ha.

Within this framework I was really confident about the magazine though. And the one thing that killed me when doing it was that somebody else was meant to produce it, then somebody else was meant to manage the distribution and the sales … which they weren't doing. People were just taking things, taking all the money. So I had to do all of that myself. I was going to the post office full time and sending every single PayPal order myself. I would write a personal reply to the actual person and it was taking up all of my time. But when I think about it now, what's cool is that I was writing to some academic from Houston, or a hipster from Bangkok. I can probably still look through my PayPal history. It's really weird the types of people who were buying it, and every now and then I'd ask someone: How did you find out about this? People were saying to me: Look, you've got to narrow down your target audience and this and that. Obviously I was getting a lot of 'aesthetic philosophical thrill' doing this but the workload was huge. Plus I'm really difficult with people; it's not fun. Making a magazine is crazy shit and everybody wants to be your friend and everybody kind of hates you and people go crazy. About five people that I know of took off with the magazine's [*F de C Reader*] content and retitled/rebranded it themselves. People get upset.

RCo Can I ask you about Japan? About how it shows you, to a degree, what's happening in the rest of the world. I wonder whether you felt that in Perth because everything …

AH Oh in a different way. Yeah. Japan is like a series of time capsules. They preserve Tang dynasty clothes and still wear them; all the vintage American denim and Italian bicycle parts. Then there's the micro-booms that show you a bullet-size version of something that's going on elsewhere. Like ... coriander and the superflat psychology or non-psychology. Didn't [Jacques] Lacan freak out because the Japanese people don't have a sub- or un-conscious? That itself kind of lays bare all of human psychology, when you realise that the Japanese psyche is no different to any other.

RC I mean it's almost like the polar-opposite to Perth. That sense of always being a performer when you're in public space.

AH Definitely. Japan has practically no public space. My ideal has been for a long time, to spend half the year in Tokyo, and half in Perth. That would be perfect because either of those places becomes too much for longer than six months, and less time is not enough. Perth definitely did something to me in ways that I've yet to think about. It was like a shock, and I was shocked to the point that I didn't feel it. The imag I had of Perth and the reality of getting there were very different; I thin I went into a state of amnesia, literally. I was in London, and European have this image of the beaches in Australia, and I'm looking at the ma of Perth and I thought it was going to be something like Rio, and tha this long thing called 'The Boulevard' is going to be like a boulevard i Paris. I was still a teenager but this was the image I had. So when I lande there, yeah, it was quiet. But after living in Romania and Germany and I've also lived in England and Sweden – things were pretty toug for Eastern Europeans. So Western Australia by comparison felt reall normal. I felt at home. I was not the weirdo lesser Eastern Europea being. So that was ok.

RCo How old were you when you left Romania?

AH Seventeen, technically sixteen.

RCo And you left by yourself, right? On the train?

AH With my mother. Yeah by train. We left with passport the easy way – or the lucky way. Most of my friends got out in mor interesting ways. A few did get shot. One way was to hide in the roo of a train. European trains had this small trapdoor above the toilet tha opens – if you can open it – into an attic of sorts. Some are pretty room some tiny. They're always fibreglass inside, so you'd itch and bleed fo days. In part to make up for my too-easy exit, I moved around tha way a lot myself, after I realised that Germany wasn't for me and I ha destroyed my useless Eastern European passport. I spent many night at border police stations in countries that were to soon become the co EU countries.

Funny you mention it, because the other day this scen which for some reason I had blocked out of my mind, came back to m first thing in the morning. As we were waiting for the Orient Express t leave the communist bloc in this small chemical town – Europe's mos polluted at the time, even your toothpaste would go black if you le the cap off – there were these massive stacks, about four meters tall, c wooden crates filled with live snails. I assume they were meant to go t Paris as it's the final destination of the Orient Express. But due to typic logistics at the time, they got left there on the platform longer than the should have been, so the snails cracked the boxes open and started th exodus, as far as the eye could see, towards the forest. There was th meter thick biomass near the boxes with piles of crushed shells aroun the train tracks. Quite a sight, in a [Andre] Tarkovsky kind of way. I mea everything was actually moving at snail speed.

RC You mentioned *Purple* and *Doingbird* before. Does that form of fashion art/culture magazine seem potentially viable anymore?

AH I really don't think so. Not a format like *Purple* and not righ now. But in a few years, maybe that will change. There are still a lot c magazines that look like *Purple*.

RCo Don't you think so? Because *Purple* is now a hard cover book that comes out twice a year or something, and costs $80. When do you think *Purple* stopped being interesting? Was it when Jeff Rian left? I mean he still writes for them, but …

AH I don't know if *Purple* stopped being interesting. I've been following Olivier [Zahm]'s Instagram.

RCo Olivier. I find him unbearable.

AH I think Olivier himself still has something. But the *Purple* thing has gone beyond that. That whole culture is ridiculous, it's gone way beyond pathetic. I'm sure the magazine is interesting as far as the magazine goes, but I think the reader's mind has changed. We have to figure out what we are and what we need. This is stuff that I need to think about and I want to think about eventually. But I haven't actually held a paper book in my hand for years and years. I'm sure books and paper, and even magazines and stuff are not going to die though. And social media doesn't replace them either.

RCo So maybe the thing that I mean about *Purple* is that as a form it weighs like three kilos, it's stupidly heavy. It has a weight that it never had before. There was a provisional nature to it for the first bunch of years; it felt like it was trying something out. And then you have *Purple Sex*, *Purple Fiction*, *Purple*-whatever, and everything is sitting within a thing, and very certain. Some of the writing and some of the shoots are still kind of open, but it seems to have lost that sense of the provisional, the testing, the trying something out.

AH Oh for sure.

RCo The provisional seems to be integral to your stuff. I'm wondering about this because when you were making these kind of things, I think you were doing the *Live Journal* as well?

AH Oh *Live Journal*. Yeah.

RCo For me that was one of the greatest ways to encounter your work because there was an immediacy to it. You were shuffling stuff around I guess. It was exactly what it said – a 'live journal' – and it felt like just that. I wonder whether you miss that platform and whether the live journal and printed publications you were doing around that time were carrying that spirit across into a paper form?

AH I honestly don't miss anything from any time. At the moment, I feel a particular way because Tokyo is very much like Instagram, and everything is just overloaded. I have a couple of friends, more like comrades, who are photographers. There's Anders [Edstrom], who, it struck me, takes massive and equal responsibility and care for every image he makes, and that's really amazing. I think we really need to start looking and going in that direction. Sure, every serious photographer has their archive, and you even keep your lousy stuff, because one day you might see something different in it. Anders does it differently – in a way I'm only just beginning to comprehend, easy as it may sound. It's basically an ecological thing, much like taking responsibility for, or at least being properly conscious of, the garba you produce and every part of the animal or vegetable you kill f food. But few humans I think are capable of doing that in the realm images. I do it in a more intense way, but Anders is more methodic He really stands behind taking responsibility for every single ima that he takes. There's a whole new way that we can look at images a deal with things. I think there's some really exciting stuff to come. Th there's this other guy who's more strategic perhaps, who sees imag making as a subtractive act. For him photography is a way to take aw a photo. I think there's a lot to that. I guess, again, that's like maki a space. This guy really believes that and I believe it too. Every act taking a photo is actually removing a whole slice from this overload world of images.

RC To clarify, when you say every photo takes away, are you saying that t photo takes away the saturation of Instagram and the mass of images? Which is super paradoxical way of saying …

AH I have been doing this in my own way, but I can't quite p down what I'm doing and how I'm doing it. I don't do things like the guys. But there are different ways in which you can take away or cle up. I have argued with Anders a few times about this. It took him a lo time to come up with his idea of *weak images*. Everybody wants to ma strong images. He likes the weak image, which I think is kind of bullsh because that image itself is strong in its own way – or in his own wa because he is a bit of an institution. Fundamentally there are two way you can go into the vague, the nothing, the fuzzy; or you can go into t whack, into the obvious. You can take away.

In a way, that's how I think about the reader. The covers a so ridiculous that you – by doing that right – can clear out 500 imag with one. You just empty them out. I've never been worried abo doing stereotypical cliché stuff. So you go straight into the obvious nothing. I think all art does that. From there, it's hard to actually put in words, but there's a great point where pictures just talk to each oth and people who see, just see it. There's probably something really co that's going to happen. We've got AI [artificial intelligence] and tha going to take over this and that but what about the images themselve They have their own lives. They do. They exist. And I think they're mo intelligent or they've been fed more human intelligence than the A This sounds kind of like mystical bullshit, but I think it's here that there a lot of stuff happening.

If I think about it now, those ex-soviet bloc designers lik Demna Gvasalia at Balenciaga have done just that. It's neither quotin nor subverting. Nor is it just 'memes', it's something new. It's easy to sa like Hito Steyerl, that it's just capital grabbing everything for itself b the quickest possible means, but that leaves out too much to actual make sense.

RCo I like that idea so much: the lifeworld of the image. One coherent imag can take away the stress from all the other images that might have taken that spac because now that space is occupied. It's like the Tetris theory of images. If you've g this image, then no other images need to go there anymore. I like the agency with that, the piling up and the sifting and the antique movement of it all. And then the notion of taking equal responsibility for each photograph and how that takes away from the teleological idea of a narrative that is building towards a larger outcome. I don't want to sound too cheesy in segueing back to *IOU*, but I'm interested in that sense of ongoing equivalence. So when you were laying this out, was there a sense of balancing out?

AH When making art, I don't know what I'm doing or why I'm doing it, so there's an extra sort of thrill or inevitability. If I know why I'm doing it and what it means, then it's not art; it's just some job I'm doing. The fridge in the photos, if you look here [in his Tokyo apartment] it's a similar kind of fridge to mine. I'm using both the front and the back of this fridge. The back makes heat which is good if you ferment – I make a lot of rice wine and stuff. I'm re-using and making good use of energy, not wasting it. The electricity bill here is about $10 a month. This fridge creates both coolness and warmth. So it definitely relates to that. At the time I made *IOU*, I wasn't thinking, Oh, I'm going to reinvent the fridge by taking that photo. Yet it's all there. Like there is a technical kind of thing. I also worked for four years in a tofu factory in Melbourne, and I can show you pictures of tofu that look like stuff in that book. They all make equal sense to me. And it's basically all the stuff of life, same with the bicycles, this and that. What I'm trying to say, especially now, looking at that book, is that it's very much a technical thing: a manual or users' guide of sorts. And it extends to this moment. Over the past five to 10 years I've been really into science and coding. I did electronics in high school and I've always had this sort of technical side. I don't see it as secondary to any other skill; that's the Renaissance thing – the metaphorical/visual and the scientific/technical both lead to the same thing. I'm very much into doing things thoroughly, properly.

RC What code are you writing?

AH At the moment I'm really looking into the Unix shell itself. You can do so much in just that.

RCo I've literally no idea what that is or does.

AH You're using a Mac?

RCo Yeah.

AH Well, if you go to the terminal, it's the language you use there. I've got a hell of a lot of threads to bring together. Because in the nineties I was also really into web design and I was struggling to find my place in the world. I was more drawn to coding than to visual design. But there was a limit to how deep I wanted to go, or could go, because I have a photographer's brain, always looking to be surprised or overwhelmed. There is definitely no control, at least in the photography that I do; whereas coding is all about control. So, yeah, now they're all coming together as one piece.

RCo You asked before we started about why we didn't email the questio for this interview. I'm pleased we did it this way because we're going to see th thing about language come through – the thing that is supporting the device tha communicating what you're/we're 'in' at this point. And then there's the notion metaphor – the thing that speaks about something that doesn't speak about it; tha a kind of vehicle in a particular way. And then the making of a space and the spac being the platform for the thing.

AH I hope you can find something.

RC Yeah. There's something beautiful.

(02) Alin Huma

The collaborative artist's book *IOU* (2003) documents a series of situations between photographer-publisher Alin Huma and dancer-performer Cheiko Kawaguchi. The work charts the unfolding of various scenarios in which each player acts out roles, behind or in front of the camera, with different props and in a range of contexts. Their gestures are loaded but indeterminate and arguably presented to show that a photograph might entail a social encounter when the notion of distribution and reproducibility hovers over it. The title *IOU* expands this idea to suggest a debt between people, observing how the transactional nature of form and meaning are performed in specific social, environmental and interpersonal contexts. In this sense the photograph conditions both the action and the response.

Alin Huma was born in Romania in 1968. He currently lives and works in Tokyo. Huma has exhibited and published internationally, including presentations at Sibiu, Romania (2004); Gertrude Contemporary, Melbourne (2007); and Yadoya, Tokyo (2007). In 2012, his work was featured in Hijacked III: Contemporary Photography from Australia & the UK at the Australian Centre for Photography, Sydney; Perth Institute of Contemporary Arts; and The Quad, Derby.

Cheiko Kawaguchi was born in 1976 in Japan. Maintaining a solo practice as a dancer/performer, Kawaguchi has previously collaborated with Alin Huma on several projects including *IOU*, the artist book and large-scale photo installation made for the exhibition mix tape at the Art Gallery of Western Australia in 2004.

We become per–formative objects of language

This conversation took place via Zoom on 9 December 2020 between Jani Ruscica i Helsinki and Rachel Ciesla and Robert Cook in Boorloo/Perth.

RC Could we begin by talking about your video *Human Flesh* [201 exhibited here in the BODIED exhibition: how did the work come into being in general sense? It is clear that your practice explores language in breadth and deta And that seems to be what you're doing in this piece also. But can you talk abou where this work sits for you?

JR I have been working with anthropomorphic fonts for qui a few years, in woodcuts and other mediums, and I'd been exploring th relationship between the image and the object, and how that transitio or translation operates in my earlier works. *Conversation in Pieces* [201 and *Flatlands* [2018] are sort of performative sculptural works whe the objects are activated, and they're interpreted and recontextualise through the performances, and through the invitation to perform interact with them. So, in *Human Flesh* I guess I extended out fro that, as well as my interest in anthropomorphic fonts and their histor and the use of the body and performance. I had also seen a project b a French studio who produced these experimental fonts of their studi staff shaped into fleshy, lumpy figures which have a resemblance to typographic sign. That really was the trigger in a way, and I felt th I articulated this relationship between the sign and the body furth in many ways.

RC One of the things about the piece is that the mouth is very presen Are you thinking in terms of how language also structures the body that is speaking it

JR Yes, absolutely. I think that was one of the core interest and how the language – maybe that's what you mean by 'structures' places that body and how it also determines a body and multiplicit But I guess, even in more general terms, I'm always interested in th moment of recognition, when it's unstable somehow; when you have t question what you are recognising. I think it relates to naming and cate gorising. There is an instability there, in simple day-to-day terms; thing aren't easy to fix in place. Meaning is not as easy to fix as we assume.

RCo Do you have a particular interest in the philosophy of language and Lacanian psychoanalysis? Or do you intuitively explore the fissures and confusions between language, experience and naming, as you work through them?

JR I have had an interest in semiotics, but my educational background has been more in media theory; I've been through [Gilles] Deleuze, Marshall McLuhan and others. I'm also interested in recent discourse including post humanism and cyber feminism. At the moment I'm reading Legacy Russell's *Glitch Feminism*. In a more contemporary context, I am asking what does that mean and how does it resonate? So I think it's a mix of influences, and in recent years I've come back to what I read twenty years ago.

RCo Yes, I think I'm doing the same and I'm just going to pick up a book on Rachel's desk – Simone Weil's *Gravity & Grace*.

JR You're going back to the classics too.

RC Yes, I picked this book up because I was thinking about the tap dancer in *Human Flesh* and Morse code. The idea of the two people being in a cell separated by a wall which they communicate through by tapping. It's about that mode of connection. And I was interested in the ways people connect through language and gesture and sound in your work. So what I'm picking up in relation to Simone Weil is your interest in code, and also the necessity to communicate.

JR Yes, and I'm also working with misinterpretation and miscommunication in many ways because – maybe it's my bi-cultural background – I've always felt that there's been a sort of struggle to identify things without fully understanding one's own cultural context. So that also resonates with the idea of attempting to communicate, but often finding it difficult or challenging. With the tap piece in *Human Flesh*, I started off with the poetry, because I felt poetry's use of language has a logic that is always challenging language beyond the literal. It operates in the gaps, in the interstices. Now I'm developing a version of that piece in which I'm working with even more abstract ways of using language; where it's just the syllables. I felt like I needed to introduce an element of chance, so, for the next exhibition I'm doing, all the invigilators will be wearing tap shoes. It is a sort of a soundscape and a reading, which is very much up to chance.

RCo That sense of breaking words down into syllables is one thing poetry does; it creates a rhythm so that another kind of meaning happens. It seems like this is what you were doing when you were constructing hybrid musical instruments that played different scales. Is it your notion that language can operate in these ways to generate meanings that are felt on different levels and can't be articulated very clearly?

JR Yes. I think that's a sort of primary stand, and it's also a bit of a paradox because often I find people relating to my work as very layered and dense with references. Which, of course, takes it back to language definitions and the fact that it's defined through language. In a way it's contradictory to define the very content, or the core of my practice, as language, when actually it's the inability of language articulate certain meanings that is central.

RCo How is your training as a sculptor informing your work nov It seems there might be connections to the work of Robert Morris or Donald Juc in terms of its physicality and the creation of particular relationships that can't b decoded in a narrative sense. It feels like what you're doing is working with the *ca* of placement and considering how that shapes someone's relationship; and throug this that you are creating a space to honour those felt experiences. Your work shak open the need to *know*, to definitively say 'this means that and that means this'. An there's a sculptural element that's core to this resistance.

JR I think it's interesting that you mention people like Donal Judd and Robert Morris. It's their sort of work that I've been ve interested in but have never felt an affinity with. It's never been somethir which I could naturally relate to my practice. Maybe in recent yea I related to ideas of minimalism and it's kind of performative space, b I don't think I've articulated that in my head. It's something which I' learned to read in work by sculptors like Judd and Morris by revisitir their work. So yes, that aspect is definitely there. I think that placeme and care is a structure that I have deliberately worked with since my ve early practice. I often work with parallels and what emerges throug the relationship of placement. And funnily enough, I've worked wit performative works – it's odd that I call them performative even thoug they are sculptural – like *Flatlands* and *Conversation in Pieces*. Ofte this placement happens through the medium of video, like in *Scer Shifts* [2012] where I looked at artefacts and objects which have specific cultural resonance. I've worked again with ways of complicatin that straightforward visual perception through the use of language sound to create a sort of parallel or contradictory reading.

RCo Can we go back to something you mentioned before abou your bi-cultural position in relation to this parallel, contradictory quality? When wer you aware of the 'constructedness' of language and the precariousness of meaning Was this present for you very early in life?

JR I think so. I mean psychologically, I always related back several personal experiences and living between two very different on a European scale – cultural identities. I also don't think of gend or sexuality as fixed or stable categories. Everything is related to th way I always wanted to not define things, and I think that's somethin which reads in my practice. So yes, that was there very early on. Living i two places [Finland and Italy], and being bilingual, made me understan that. I was always equally strong in both languages, and so I saw ho relative meaning was – how it could so easily shift and how it could b misinterpreted. I think that's sort of it, but I don't know at what poir it found its way into my practice. I've never specifically thought abou at what point that happened. In my own personal career, I was goin to train as a musician. Like a lot of artists, I have always drawn an painted from a very early age, but until I was 17 or 18 I was plannin to be an oboist. And I shifted from that. I sort of went back. So I thin I have always been negotiating different kinds of languages and ho they relate to each other. How they translate from one to the other. That process has always existed for me.

RCo You mentioned the oboe, and as we said before, the focus in *Human Flesh* is very much on mouths. How were you shaping or choreographing the performances in that specific regard?

JR You know, in the past I'd always really resisted using professional actors in any of my works. A lot of the works haven't had a human presence, so they weren't acted as such. Maybe there was a voiceover. But in this work, that was essential because these *formed-forms* were so static. They were kind of tactile, obviously fleshy in some way, but in terms of movement, they were just very static. So I needed to activate them, because it's not only the linguistic content but the expression of the language with shapes that's important. I needed to really play with the expression: How many ways can you say a specific word, and how does that shape or change the meaning? I ended up working with professional actors and actually shot them in pairs, like they appear in the video, so they would bounce off each other. I had written something, but then we just filmed it and they kept improvising and adding to it as well. I really wanted them to play with that dialogue because in most scenes there are two figures – two characters – so that's how it was actually made. The only things that were extracted from their faces were the eyes and the mouths, so expression is limited to these features.

RC Can you talk about how you see the relationship of sex and gender to language, and how this sits in the work for you? I'm thinking about this pairing, for example, and the use of the word 'fuck'.

JR Well, obviously there are signifiers in the work that identify a voice as gendered. The piece really speaks about the performativity of language, and that obviously has a strong relationship to gender and sexuality as well. It's a part of that discussion about identifying things, and how unstable, restrictive, simplistic or inadequate language can be in doing that. 'Fuck' just felt like, well, there is the 'F' of flesh, so it was one of the 'power words' to be used. In that figure it is also used to voice some kind of frustration like she's trying to say something and she's unable to say it. There's f-fear, f-f-fear, f-f-f-fear, you know.

RC That sense of frustration and the inability to articulate feels particularly resonant, it's so palpable. It really taps into your thinking because each character uses language to speak about the different ways that we might express ourselves through gender, sex or power. Each of these relations – at certain times and between certain characters – ebb and flow throughout the work. There is this paradoxical element where the linguistic content shapes the expression – the way you hold your tongue in your mouth in order to speak a particular word – but then equally your expression works in the opposite way because it will have an impact on the linguistic content – the volume or tone of your words will change their meaning. And there is the coding and the decoding. Morse code, or any code, works because someone is able to understand it or interpret it, and others are not. Everything is both inclusionary and exclusionary.

JR Yes, I've always been interested in those aspects of language I've often revisited it, especially in the work *Scene Shifts* which has several languages spoken in it. In that piece from 2011, I didn't even want to use subtitles because I thought that it activates us in a different way if we can't understand the linguistic content but we're still able to hear the language. But then I decided that would have been too extreme, too excessive, because the work included quite a few different languages and that would be too limiting.

RC When you are making the videos, especially *Human Flesh*, do you storyboard very precisely? Do you also do all the filming? How do you address the animation and how does the editorial process work?

JR I work with a cinematographer and a team that might change from project to project. *Human Flesh* was very clearly planned beforehand because there are no edits; it's basically a single take Even though it was shot in separate parts and was pieced together in post-production, it was choreographed because the characters spelled out the words 'human flesh'. I made sketches of the material that I would shoot with the actors, and I drew these characters which a 3D designer then made according to my plans. I also edited and scripted them, but as I said, I allowed for quite a bit of improvisation. I kind of prioritised the expression over the content or the words. So that's pretty much the process. It was very labour-intensive in terms of post-production and getting the rhythm to work, and because it allowed so little room for adjustments. You would usually have much more freedom in the editing process; you could shift things around, you could cut things. Here none of that was allowed. I could only use single takes which worked as a whole. And the 3D designer nearly had a nervous breakdown. I mean I nearly had a nervous breakdown as well, because it was so hard to fit them into the shapes and he would say, 'You have to reshoot everything These people are moving too much and it's too expressive; you have to contain it more.' And I would say, 'No, but I can't, it has to be expressive and lively.' But in the end I think we managed to solve the problems and make the work together.

RC Were you thinking a lot about the duration of the video – I think it's fifteen minutes – as well? Do you think that the duration is important in terms of its demand on an audience's attention span?

JR I don't think it's intentional – or perhaps on a subconscious level it is. I've made works up to 25 minutes long. I do think of my primary context as the gallery space. So I guess in those terms, I must be thinking about what is a reasonable amount of time for something to work as a looping piece. Even though *Human Flesh* has a clear beginning and end I still think of it as just looping. I allow the material to kind of express what it needs; I try to work with that.

RCo The looping makes the video mirror or mimic itself as it goes around It's interesting in the context of this exhibition as a whole, as all the other works are three minutes maximum, so yours is the longest piece. Everything else is like a pop song and yours is like the extended play at the end.

JR Actually, a lot of my colleagues seem to work with an extended sort of film essay format in which 45 minutes isn't very long at all. So in relation to that, I think working with 10 to 20 minutes is quite a short, brief format. And because I'm working with this kind of episodic structure, even though *Human Flesh* is a single take, it has these very distinctive vignettes. So, I think there also needs to be enough of them to have a dialogue with each other. I could have had more objects – but I only had the lemonade glass, the lamp and the drone. I'm often trying to negotiate what is enough and what is too much. And when you're working with video, you have to think of dramaturgy as well, and about whether to make the experience excruciatingly long or slow.

RC There is a moment with the tap-dancer when it teeters on the edge of unbearable. When you think maybe its gone on slightly too long ... I don't believe it does but it does brush up against that boundary.

JR I'm a big fan of works by artists like Sharon Lockhart or Tacita Dean. I remember watching, *Pine Flat* [2006], Lockhart's film in the theatre at MoMA [New York]. And at the end of the screening there were only four of us left because each vignette is the length of the 16-millimeter film roll. So it's about 11 minutes and there are maybe 15 of them. And they're static shots in which nothing really happens. It's around 150 minutes of just watching these 10-minute still lives. I really liked that – that she extended and also forced the viewer into this really different frame of mind in a meditative space.

RCo Can you talk a little about your choice of the Alto lamp and the drone?

JR I just used industrial design, architecture, and the objects we interact with and engage with in our daily lives.

RCo So you've never been making specific references to, or offering a particular take on, Modernism?

JR No, not particularly, because I might be equally interested in a Memphis object or an art deco object. I don't place so much emphasis on eras, I'm interested primarily in the mimetic qualities of these objects. But I have to say, I am working on several things and I'm quite slow at forming these relationships. I might form a relationship between objects not only within a single work, but also within a whole body of works. I find this problematic at times because one piece might suggest a reading about an interesting modernist form, but within the whole, it is part of a broad range of sources and objects.

RCo You mentioned Deleuze earlier. Could you extrapolate from what you were saying about returning to a fragment of an older work, and then using that as a platform to make new connections? In your work there is this sense of moving backward and forward, and not tying it down. One artwork is not a stationary, unitary thing, but is connecting in and out. Is that how you see your practice?

JR Yeah, absolutely. I think it relates to shifting from working predominantly with video. I felt video was somehow really fixed in this way and that I could form other relationships too. That's why I reall wanted to return to sculpture and objects, and to these performativ objects, because I felt they weren't as fixed. They had the capacity t transform much more fluidly and freely into other things. Also, b subjecting them to somebody else's reading or interpretation. I quit literally meant to do that, and I think it's a very important element of m practice. I guess I'm not thinking necessarily about something being lik a puppet, though obviously it's a performative object. I think we becom performative objects of language.

RC You have used puppets or types of puppets a few times in differen modes. How did you find that particular form? People like Wael Shawkey have don amazing things with puppetry, but it could almost be a kind of taboo for an artist.

JR I think I worked with puppets for the first time in 2004 I was still in college and I worked with Sicilian puppetry because it's traditional form of puppetry that I had seen throughout my life, an I had several of those puppets. And then it wasn't until *Conversation i Pieces*, because that work is also about *appropriation* – and I think that' maybe something we haven't tapped into so much – as well as mimicr and the circulation of images and material. It's all part of that interestin transformation or shift in assigning meaning. In *Conversation in Piece* my point of reference was [Luigi] Pirandello's play *Six Characters i Search of an Author* [1921]. I was thinking of the objects in quite simila terms, and the piece was created by appropriating existing material an working with and reworking the cultural histories that they imply, o that they embody in some way as objects. I was obviously dealing wit issues of authorship as well. And that's why I included a ventriloquis puppet head of myself in order to place myself within that chain o authorship. I dared to use puppetry only in response to my question relating to authorship and whose voice is being spoken.

RCo I guess we could see puppets operating in the same way as musica instruments in your work and within the broader idea of a performative objec And maybe that's also what I had in my mind with Robert Morris – the idea of th person inside the box. While we're picking up the idea of circulation of meaning an authorship, where do you see the future of language going? Have you even though about that? For instance right now we're speaking in English. Accents are shifting given how media works, and accents are obviously important in your work.

JR Even though there's English in my work, I do use a lo of Finnish as well, and in *Human Flesh* there is also Italian and othe languages. I really try to resist the shift to everything being only i English. And of course, in the woodcuts I work with this because I titl them in English and so when you translate them it doesn't make sens anymore. If I'm exhibiting in Italy, then U for ultramarine becomes U fo oltremare, which is O actually. That is something I find really interestin in these works, and I like it when it actually doesn't work anymore. Th title doesn't work when translated. I've been here [in Helsinki] for th past year working as a professor at the Academy of Fine Arts and th shift to English really does worry me; everything is actually taught i English and there's barely any content in Finnish. I mean, who woul speak Finnish now? Obviously, no one, unless you lived here all your life. It worries me how it narrows meaning. Of course it's such a complex question; such a complex web on a cultural level. It's quite interesting that I've only once in my life lived in a place where I didn't know the language and that was the Netherlands. I didn't know any Dutch and it was also a language that I had absolutely no understanding of. And I felt like I had no entry point into the culture either. I really struggled to understand on many levels. So in that sense language can deny access, and you can clearly exclude in quite violent ways as well. But of course, I do recognise the importance of language. As much as I have talked about its inadequacy and instability, it is an undeniable fact that we can't understand phenomena unless we try to create a language to speak about them.

(03) Jani Ruscica

Jani Ruscica's video *Human Flesh*, 2019, has an elegantly minimal feel that sits between the white walls of an art gallery and the clinical surfaces of a scientific laboratory. Concerned with the phenomenon of language, the video's communicative capacity, as well as its existential sounds and shapes, feels like a deliberate experiment conducted into the weirdness of the human operating system. Animated letters with human voices and faces spell out the work's title. As if trying on their forms for the first time, these characters sensuously make us aware of the intimate relationship between our biological reality and the culture that binds and divides us. Our language comes into being through the specific capacities and limitations of the human body, which it then shapes in turn.

Jani Ruscica was born in 1978 in Savonlinna, Finland, raised in Italy and is currently based in Helsinki. They obtained an MFA from the Finnish Academy of Fine Arts, Helsinki in 2007 and a BFA from Chelsea College of Art and Design, London in 2002. They have realised a wide range of collaborations and commissions, including for Camden Art Centre and Animate Projects in London; MoMA PS1, Creative Time and MTV global in New York. Their work was included in the 1st Riga Biennial (2018); and presented at the Kiasma Museum of Contemporary Art, Helsinki (2016); and the Kunsthalle Detroit, Museum of Contemporary Art (2013).

My body as a domestic object

This conversation took place via Zoom on 26 January 2021 between Kawita Vatanajyankur in Bangkok and Rachel Ciesla and Robert Cook in Boorloo/Perth.

RC In this exhibition there's an open conversation between your work and Cheryl Donegan's that acknowledges a lineage of performative feminist practice. Can we start with a consideration of how you began to explore those concerns?

KV The works in BODIED are from a series I made when I first came back to Thailand from Australia. Surprisingly, it's a series that I've continued to develop for the past nine or 10 years; even as I have moved onto other projects, I've continued to use my body as a domestic object. There were of course elements of this approach when I was living in Australia, and I was adjusting into a culture that I was unfamiliar with. I felt like I was in two worlds, Australia and Thailand. I think I have always been an outsider or an alien. Growing up in Thailand as a child and then moving to Australia as a teenager, I felt like I had to objectify myself in order to fit into society, but, even so, I would never be a 'true Australian'. And coming back to Thailand I was once again an outsider within Thai society. The roles or expectations relating to behaviour are very prescribed, especially for women; I had to always consider what I should say and express to be a 'good woman' in Thailand.

In other words, when I came back to Thailand, it was like I had to grow up again. I was about 23 or 24 and was starting new relationships with the culture, the environment, friends, family and romantic partners. I had to figure out how to fit into a society that made me feel like a child again and this required me to fully objectify myself. It made me question my value. In Australia, I'd learned to express what I feel, to speak up, and stand up for myself. But when I came back to Thailand I was covered by the 'container' of what a woman should be. I was a liquid being put into the container. And so I started to reflect on that, I transformed my body into various tools and objects within the house. I was also struck at the time by the word 'domesticated' because it is not just about being in the house, or doing all the actions of cleaning the house; it's also about making yourself comply, obey, and not be 'you'– to be some-thing else that they think that you should be. So I started to act as various objects. In *Soaked* [2012] my body is being used as a mop, and in *The Ice Shaver* [2013] I'm shaving a block of ice with my head to create the ice flakes for a traditional Thai dessert.

RC After you've done a performance like that, and you've shot it, does that sense of being a tool or being erased stay with you afterwards?

KV When I performed *The Ice Shaver* I completely transformed myself. I entered the work as myself, as a human being – my face was almost frozen from the coldness of the ice and I felt a sense of pain – but then as time went by (this video is about three or four minutes long) there was a transition from human to object. My face was numb and I felt less and less a sense of self, in terms of a being or feeling. Then, both physically and psychologically, I was transformed into a complete object.

This is also the result of practicing for the performances. Sometimes it takes me about two to four weeks to be able to complete the action for the entire duration of the piece. I can't just go and do a new performance; I wouldn't be able to. I would fall or give up in the first minute or two because of the challenge I have to face. Some tasks are easier than others, but many are very hard to do. Mostly, I can do only one or two minutes at the start. The next day I can do five minutes. I practice until I can endure it for long enough to do the final shoot. And after a while I am still that object. I still think of it now; I think of the endurance. I think that kind of endurance has stayed with me forever. The limitations of my endurance have been extended.

RC You have people 'assisting' you in the videos. Who is the woman in the other works? Is that your mother or a friend or family member?

KV Most are family members, like my mother; and sometime its my housekeeper. My housekeeper is also my inspiration. She gave me a lot of ideas for my earlier works, and my later works about labour as well. In a lot of the works, she created equipment or props for me or constructed the studio, or helped with the actions. So she is my collaborator actually.

RC How does she see the work? Because in a way it's a critique of that type of labour that she's involved in? And how does your mother see the work from her perspective?

KV In every work that I've done with my housekeeper or with other women who are constructing the equipment or building the studios with me, I think they see it as valuing their hard, difficult work. It's regarded as an abstract thing, ignored and not seen within society. The work called *Plough (Plow)* [2020], is performed by myself and two other women. One is a machine or an animal, the other is a plough that is adjusting the soil. My face was being dragged through the soil and I was falling and coming up again. There was a moment in that project when the other women both cried.

After that I started to also look at how the invisible labour occurring within the house is only a tiny part of a large systematic problem within society. The workers behind mass production are abstract. They are the ones at the bottom of the hierarchy, working behind closed doors. My series *Field Work* [2020] explores how humans are being objectified and dehumanised by a society of capitalism based on materialism. The series is geared towards questions of equity and equality, and I'm researching the factories and looking inside the fruit markets to see the labourers behind all these productions. And ther are so many women, for instance, within the local markets in Thailand, who are working almost like tools in a machine. My family (except for my mum and my dad) are all lawyers, so I have the scales of justice everywhere, just lying around my house. I have seen them since I was very young and I think they have been a constant reminder of questions about whether fairness is real within the current system of capitalism.

Doing my own research into labour practices I found that Thailand has one of the highest rates of human trafficking and labour exploitation in the world, especially in the fishing industry. I did a series called *Splashed* [2017] where the body is a carrier or a large net which is going down into the blue ocean and carrying the saltwater fish up and down, up and down. Many documentaries show how labourers in the fishing industry are being treated as human nets. These human nets are being locked within the boat at night, sleeping on top of each other, and then forced to work for many hours. Sometimes they work for three days in a row without sleeping to catch as many fish as they can for the seafood exporter. I really wanted to research that series further, but my aunt, an attorney, warned me that it is very dangerous because law and policies do not cover activities offshore.

Around that time, I also went to several factories in both Thailand and India, and started talking to the labourers there. While I was in Bangalore, the female textile and garment workers were protesting against the government because their wages were so low that they couldn't survive. During the protest I saw a woman holding a sign that said 'Are we machines?'. There are many protests in Thailand as well as Bangalore, Bangladesh and Cambodia, where these workers are demonstrating for their rights, for their own voice, for more wages so that they can survive. Most of the time they are being pushed back violently by the government or the police, and their treatment never makes it to the news. I really wanted to unmute their voices.

RCo You do this in a sense by acting it out. In this regard, do you agree that your works are becoming more complex in relation to both industrial and mythological connections?

KV Yes. At one of the knitting factories, I saw a weaving room that had a very large circular loom. The needle in the middle was going around and around to create a tube of fabric. It inspired me to incorporate this element into my live performance *The Spinning Wheel* [2018]. In this work I am the needle that is going around, and I am using my whole body, especially my legs and my mouth to bite and to knit the tube of fabric. Towards the end of this performance it is almost like I am knitting a spider web. And so I reflected a little more on the story of Arachne who was a weaver that was turned into a spider so she has to continually spin thread. Athena set a test for her because she felt that Arachne insulted the power of the gods, and so she was turned into a spider as punishment for not following what the higher beings demanded. I see a connection between my work and myself as a human spider who is forever knitting a web, like Arachne. Knitting is a form of work, a form of labour, but also a form of survival. To perform this work, I must use all parts of my body like the spider with its eight legs – I am being that machine. I first performed the work at the Bangkok Art

Biennale and then in Abu Dhabi during the Culture Summit and then Taipei [at Project Fulfill Art Space].

RC The performance is roughly half an hour long?

KV Yes, but sometimes it's an hour. The first time it took a hour, but I think I got more efficient at performing the action.

RCo Your work is so rigorous and detailed. It contains so much feeling ar commitment. I wonder, how do you see the body of the artist working within th political economy at this point in time?

KV Well, for me art is a soft power and I think the beauty of a is that it opens up so many possible interpretations. It's a visual languag of philosophy. There are so many analytical thoughts and feelings th you can read and experience from one piece of art. And yes, the researc is based on solid experience of going into fields and factories – it's ve direct – but when I'm making work, I am always aware that I should n make a direct message. I think that the truth or the solution does n lie in what is directly happening. My research is very grounded in th reality of this world but through art we can seek the truth that is outsic the current system or beyond the reality that we live in.

RC Is that something that the framework of your Buddhism la a platform for?

KV Yeah. I really think that it does. I started studying Buddhis when my dad passed away – more than ten years ago now – and wh I found is the truth beyond all concepts, beyond the reality. I think art is cue towards that truth because it makes people question reality. It mak people question what alternative worlds could be happening while th are seeing, interpreting, or experiencing the abstract languages in art.

RC When you were studying in Melbourne, were you thinking from th kind of perspective?

KV When I was studying in Melbourne, my dad had alreac passed away. After he died, I began reading the concepts of Buddhisr I admit it was a way for me to not suffer so much from my loss. I found very helpful and supportive in dealing with my emotions, and everythir that was happening to me. And so I use Buddhism within my work, bo in terms of philosophy and method. Most importantly, I don't know if th is perhaps a bit cheesy, but maybe it all started when I was questionir my dad's death and my loss. My father was a movie star in Thailand ar he worked as a CEO for a production house, but he was most famo for working hard. He would go on TV shows and say 'I work eight days week and I'll sleep when I'm dead'. He was a workaholic, and he believe that success would bring happiness because that's what we are value for in society. But I question that now because, before his death, he sa that he misunderstood life and it's that misunderstanding that leads death. My dad died from overworking.

(04) Kawita Vatanajyankur

As the suffering subject of her own video performances, Kawita Vatanajyankur creates and enters into situations that require her to endure physical and emotional hardship. These performances are oriented as a critical response to the experiences of women, in Thailand and globally, and the problems associated with consumerism. In *Soaked*, 2012, *Poured*, 2013, and *The Dustpan*, 2014, she places herself in the position of a domestic tool in order to act out, and painfully embody, the loss of female selfhood within the labour mechanisms of the family unit. These formations are lived day-in and day-out by billions of people as if unchangeably inevitable, and in Vatanajyankur's work they clearly and shockingly exist at the very edge of the bearable.

Kawita Vatanajyankur was born in 1987 in Bangkok where she currently resides. Since graduating from RMIT University, Melbourne, in 2011, she has exhibited at MOCA Museum of Contemporary Art, Bangkok (2020); CHAT, Hong Kong (2020); Albright Knox Art Gallery, New York (2019); Bangkok Art Biennale (2018); National Taiwan Museum of Fine Arts, Taipei (2017); Monash Gallery of Art, Melbourne (2017); Asia Triennale of Performing Arts, Melbourne Arts Centre (2017); Australian Centre for Photography, Sydney (2017); The Asian Art Biennial Taiwan (2017); and the Magazzini dell'Arsenale, 57th Venice Biennale (2017).

A happy accident

This conversation took place via Zoom on 25 November 2020 between Wong Pin in Hong Kong and Rachel Ciesla and Robert Cook in Perth.

RC When we were planning this exhibition, we had your work in mind, bu didn't know that you'd lived in Perth. It's an obvious place to start, but maybe w can begin here anyway. Curiously, in previous interviews it was said that you wer 'shipped off to Perth', almost as if it was against your will – as if you were sent here fc bad behaviour.

WP To be honest, yes, it was. But that's only because I wouldn have had the chance to study further in Hong Kong. My grades weren good and I was really lazy. My parents were pretty frustrated with m situation, and so they wanted to send me somewhere else. I guess the only knew one person outside of Hong Kong and he lived in Perth, s they sent me there. And I really don't like to make decisions or to plan a all. So I just went with their will.

RC You would have had no idea what Perth was going to be like, right?

WP No, I think I had only travelled overseas once before tha My aunt took me to America for a summer trip. So at the time that wa my only experience of places outside of Hong Kong. It was excitin because I didn't even get the chance to fly to Perth first, to feel wha it was like for a few days. I flew there and immediately started schoo when I was fifteen or sixteen.

RCo You ended up studying multimedia design at Curtin University.

WP Yes. Curtin was one of the popular schools for oversea students, and it was the first time they had multimedia, so no-one kne what was going to happen.

RCo Was it your idea to study multimedia or your parents'?

WP Definitely not their idea. I don't think they had any idea They just wanted me to have something to do rather than continue t do nothing in Hong Kong. For the first few months I studied Englis because I couldn't speak the language, and then I transferred to a hig school in Tuart Hill. I got into Curtin after a year and had no idea wha I was going to study. I saw this new course which didn't have any exam only assignments, and I thought that was fantastic, so I just took i At the time I didn't have any idea what art or drawing or design was.

RCo As the course progressed, was your focus on learning skills to get a jo in the industry, or were you thinking about ways to creatively employ what you wer learning?

WP Well, I think that was one of the differences between the west and Hong Kong. In Hong Kong it's really practical – they teach you every single button in the software. But in Perth I was more focused on developing my creative process. Learning the software was my responsibility. It's a different approach. That's why, when I finished my degree and went back to Hong Kong, I couldn't find a job because everyone else was so professional.

RCo In those early days – when you were writing stories and creating videos after-hours – was the story key to how you were observing the world around you, or were you more actively looking for a voice in which to animate and create a visual experience for people?

WP When I returned to Hong Kong, I found a job in production. But my experience of working was as a kind of suffering, so I started a blog, like in the old times before the era of Facebook. And I started writing these short stories. I didn't know what they meant, I just wrote, and it was quite organic. I didn't plan anything. And then, because of my job, I got to know the software a little better, and started using it to draw and edit. Later on, I started working with motion graphics and began making animations which I'd combine with my writing. It's similar to what I'm doing now with visuals – the colour, the shape and the movement – it's still really low-fi. Not long after that a museum commissioned me, then a gallery approached me, and that's how things roll. I didn't really have a mindset for what I was doing or what it could become.

RCo You didn't have a sense of there being any barriers to putting your work into the world? At no point were you waiting for permission?

WP The thinking was really simple. It was just my hobby. Some people play video games or play sports after work. My hobby was making animations and uploading them online for my friends to see.

RCo And you had no impulse to join the art world?

WP It was a happy accident. I still can't figure out what being an 'artist' means for my work. I tend not to think too much about what's next.

RC Did the very particular aesthetic you have – the saturated colours and the 'simple' animation – come from an interest in early computer graphics or computer games?

WP I wouldn't say they influenced me or that my design was based on them, but as a teenager everyone was enjoying video games or comics, especially in Hong Kong. It wasn't a part of my life but rather *everyone's* life. I can't tell if that was an influence, but, to be honest, I think it's the limitation of my technique. My visuals represent how much I know. I remember when I first started using the software to draw, I didn't even know how to draw a curve, I could only do sharp pointed shapes. So it was also an accident. People would say that's my style but it was only because I didn't know how to do it better.

Anyway, how did you know about me? I thought it would be because I' been in Perth ...

RC I didn't know you lived in Perth. I saw your work in London back in 201 [at The Store X]. It was the work with the police officer and his wife, *Jungle of Desir* [2015]. I saw that work and was pretty much: What the absolute fuck?!

WP It reminds you of Perth right now ... I'm kidding.

RC It is a bit like that isn't it? I mean, the overly conservative, slightly Wil West state that we are in, so it seemed fitting. Maybe that's why I gravitated toward it, because in a show of 20 video works you can get quite exhausted. And it wa maybe midway through the show. I think it was like a sigh of relief, a moment wher I could let my guard down. Yet even though your work is quite humorous on th surface, there is obviously some dense criticality in how you deal with desire an taboo. It was like getting a little bit of fresh air.

How did you feel when your work first started to be seen in the artworld You said there are no taboos anymore because on the internet everything is there, ye the art world can be heavily policed?

WP That's interesting, because production-wise I spend mor time writing than I do drawing. Sometimes I think about those concerns I might change some words, or I'll find another way to say something, bu I try not to back down too much. I also don't think political correctnes is a bad thing, but the point is rather, where is the line? I try to push th line as much as I can rather than tone it down.

I don't think much changed when I started showing i galleries. But I do get a lot of engagement in my artist talks or at th opening. Once, after an opening, a critic asked to meet up and then spen two hours telling me what I did wrong. We talked about the work calle *Who's the Daddy?* [2017] which mentions abortion. I explained to hin that I wasn't encouraging abortion but was discussing the relationshi between abortion and religion. He took it really personally and told me 'You shouldn't have said that. Why would people enjoy that?' But I d really enjoy this kind of conversation. It was different when I posted th videos online; I never had a face-to-face audience then.

RCo It's a weird moment now. The concern is not about whether things ar posted online but how they are read; everything is read very directly. And there' little consideration about whether someone might be being ironic or turning thing around. Because your work has a formal frontal quality to it – in terms of how th characters are presented, and you use subtitles or captions – there seems to be playful messaging system at work that speaks to this moment. It reads almost lik those public service announcements: it's in your best interest to look at this and stud how these people are behaving and not do that!

WP Yes, the videos seem to work on two levels. They have story but they also feel like the short film that they show before you se a movie – almost like a moral tale, telling you to watch these people an see what happens to them.

RC In *Stop Peeping* [2014], *Jungle of Desire* and *Slow Sex* [2013], you'r looking through this particular window into people's lives and taking away some kind of moral lesson. Like a fly-on-the-wall.

WP I think that's because I always referred to my writing as a diary. It was my own little social study, looking at people around me, at society. And at the same time I was reflecting on myself and my behaviour. That's why I watch so many popular movies, because I like to observe how people generally live: how they behave and particularly how they exchange words online. I always try to find the irony in these social relationships, to see the conflict in life. I would put all of this into my diary in page after page of random thoughts, and then when it came time to make the work, I would pull out everything that had happened to me over a few months and try to connect it all through one story.

One of my works *Dear, can I give you a hand?* [2018] started when I saw an old man in the park throwing away a huge black plastic bag. I waited until he left, took it out of the bin, and it was full of VHS porn tapes. It was maybe two years ago, and it had a huge impact on me because I thought: Why would he throw it out now? VHS is not used; it's not popular.

RCo Because he got a new partner?

WP [Laughs] Yes, I kept thinking, why? I ran back home and started to write a story very quickly which I made into an animation later on. So, I guess you're right about my process.

RC What elements of the work *Stop Peeping* that we're showing in BODIED are drawn from real life?

WP The whole thing, I guess. It was one of the stories from my blog. At the time, I was living in my tiny studio in an industrial building. One day the elevator was not working so I had to take the stairs. I think I lived on the fifth floor. I saw my neighbour, it was the first time I'd seen her. She was pretty and we walked from our floor to the ground floor together. We became friends and she told me she was a singer, and I was so impressed but also shocked because at that time I didn't have a job. I had to live in industrial buildings. But a young girl who is also starting her pop career lived beside me? I was shocked to learn that she also had to stay in this horrible place. She showed me her YouTube channel and she was singing and practising guitar in her room. I imagined her next door recording while I was looking at the YouTube channel. We'd hung out two or three times, and then one day I tried to see her again. I found an excuse, like borrowing an iPhone charger, and knocked on her door. And there's a naked man there. She was with the naked man, so I said: Oh! No thanks, bye. And then we didn't see each other anymore.

RCo You were so easily defeated.

WP He was naked! What can I do? But, yeah, that was the inspiration for this work.

RCo Do you know whether she saw the work?

WP I don't think so. We only briefly talked two or three time and then the last time was the door knocking and then ... no more Sometimes I would see her on TV performing, that was a few years ago but I don't know about now because I don't have a proper TV set.

RCo Sexuality is prevalent in the work and I guess you could almost only dea with that kind of material in an animated way or in a written form. But do you als think there's something inherently sexy about cartoons themselves? I'm thinking c the way figures can morph and change; that sense of the animated body being abl to expand beyond normal kinds of physicality.

WP Well, to be honest, I think cartoons and animations ar definitely sexier than the physical body. I didn't realise this at the tim but now I would say that I originally used animation to say somethin sexually terrible or violent so that people would see it as a joke. Even i I were telling a terrible story about myself – no one would really tak it seriously. In that way maybe it is sexier or more imaginative. I don' know about the audience, but I wouldn't enjoy seeing those explici scenes, if it was live action.

RC My hairdresser told me that when he first moved to Perth he got int trouble because of the more literal and direct nature of Chinese language. So I ar wondering about language and social niceties in your work, because you caption i both Cantonese and English. Is there a distinction between what you feel you ca more easily say in one language than the other? Or is it not even a consideration.

WP Oh, definitely its easier in Cantonese. I do say 'mean' stuff i Cantonese, but I hope people understand that I'm not trying to say mea things about them, but that I want to discuss something. For instance i the video *Dear, can I give you a hand?*, I was referencing the characte of the VHS man. He was an old guy and I used him to describe ho bad old people can smell sometimes. There's a difference in how yo say it. I always try to draw it back to the story rather than just ... purel ... bullying someone. That's why I spend more time writing. I try to pus the line, but not too much. I always have a hard time with this, and so th animating process is far more enjoyable for me than the writing.

RC When you are journaling and writing, does the text produce the images, c do you sometimes pull these images from life as well? Or are they sort of side by side

WP I think the process is that I separate myself into tw departments. When I am writing, I do not think about the visual. I don really care about the visuals; I just write whatever I want. And then whe I pass into my animation time, I don't think about the story, I just dra the characters. So when they come together it's never overly designe – like in *Toy Story* where the animators design the characters' emotion based on a script. That's too boring or typical for me. I prefer to have tw different brains and then just bring it together. That has chemistry.

RCo Wow! I had not actually thought of that but I can really see that being factor now. There are two things kind of floating alongside each other. How long doe it take you to write a script?

WP I would say collecting material is part of my everyday life but when I really need to write a script, maybe one to three months.

RCo So, you are doing draft after draft and then swapping out fragments and getting the pitch right?

WP Well, basically, it's just the notes on my mobile phone and then I keep changing and fine-tuning things every day. Then when I feel like 80 per cent of the script is done, I move on and start to draw and animate. I then go back to the script for a little bit more.

RCo So literally, you are writing the script on your phone?

WP Yes. Isn't it easy? I think everyone would do that nowadays.

RCo I don't write essays on my phone but I'm always tempted to. It opens up a different way of thinking for me.

WP I'm interested: do you feel like your brain works differently when you write an essay on your phone, when you use a pen, or when you're on a computer?

RCo On my phone I'm very free and I'm not worried about it. In my notebook not quite so much. And on the computer, it's like everyone's watching. That's the worst, most awful thing, because it's about finishing and a deadline. So when you're out and about, will you be taking notes if you've just seen something?

WP Nowadays I don't write it down, but I get a lot of inspiration from my Instagram stories – the instant ten seconds. They are basically my notes now. Whenever I need to sit down and start working on my script, I will just look back through my Instagram archive to see what's been happening to me. That sucks. That sounds bad.

RC No, no, no.

WP So, I'm an Instagram writer?

RCo Well, we're all Instagram curators these days. It's kind of how that works. A couple more questions, before we end though. What is your response to what's going on in Hong Kong politically and how is that shaping your work?

WP My work has always involved political and social issues in Hong Kong, or my observations of the politics in other countries. Online we basically have instant access to every political movement throughout the world. So, I don't think my art or exhibitions need to fulfil that function because Facebook and Instagram are already full of people expressing their views. But I do think it leads you to question how powerful art is in dealing with the politics in Hong Kong. I tend not to be too politically direct in my work, but I would say that politics enters the work emotionally – in how the characters are suffering or how they react.

To be honest I'm not really concerned with how overseas audiences see my work, but recently … I don't know if you know this, but people in Asia and especially Hong Kong tend to be pro-Trump. Peopl from the west would text me saying, 'What's happened to Asia? Wh are people in Hong Kong pro-Trump and how could this happen?' Wha interests me is the interaction between these different groups of peopl and how they respond to each other. My focus isn't on telling the news.

RCo To go full circle, I remember you saying that all places ar equally bad right now, so wherever you are is wherever you are. Is that how you sti feel?

WP For me, it's human nature to complain, so I would conside all places to be equally bad. For instance, during the revolution a fe years ago, a friend of mine moved from London to Hong Kong, an I asked him, 'Why would you do that?', because it was quite unstabl and the cost of living was one of the highest in the world. And he wa complaining that the art circle is so small in London, the living cost are so high, and he's frustrated with Brexit. And then he found tha everything is the same in Hong Kong but slightly worse. But I guess as foreigner, he didn't care too much because the point was to move awa from where he was. I guess I would do the same. If I moved to New Yor this week, people would be saying: No, you mustn't do it – the politic the living costs. I guess it's part of human nature to leave where yo are from so everything seems way better, but it isn't. So, in that sens I would say the world is equally bad for different people.

RC Yes, and I guess you also need friction and problems to mak your work. Your work addresses the human condition, so you need to be in a plac where it is evident. Where we're not all living a blissful, peaceful existence.

WP I find that when I travel to America or Europe, I Instagra less than when I'm staying in Hong Kong or Korea or China. The street are so crazy. It's so packed. People interact a lot and shit happen But in Europe – let's say in Basel – it's so clean and quiet; people behav I wouldn't say it's not interesting, but there's no chaos, no conflict, n contrasts for me to capture. It was interesting being there because it' supposed to make me feel that life is more enjoyable, but I don't kno that it is. Maybe I'm used to a chaotic, crowded city like Hong Kon But you're right, I need tension and conflict for my writing.

I think the tension for me is also about making a choic There is a game I used to play in which I forced myself to choos Let's say I was in an elevator, and there were four people in there, an they're all 60 or 70. I forced myself to make a choice, like decide wh I would want to have sex with. Or on the bus I'd pick one person tha I could sleep with. The game was not about turning myself on, but throug the choice I understood myself better. Let's say in the elevator, all fou of them were not my type. I still had to find the beauty in one of the and through the choice, things became clearer. I use this as an exampl but it works with social issues as well. When I create an extreme or ironi situation, I can be more honest, and so I can understand the situatio better, through choices. So the tension is more about choice for me.

(05) Wong Ping

Wong Ping's *Stop Peeping*, 2014, is a semi-surreal tale told in a high key, colour-saturated form of animation reminiscent of early video games and computer graphics. The work is based on an encounter between the artist and a young woman in his apartment block who he attempted to get to know. Over the writing process, Wong transformed this experience into a surreal meditation on loneliness and erotic connections and disconnections in crowded urban environments. In doing so, he explores situations that form when one follows the logic of observation and contact to their dramatic or logical ends.

Wong Ping was born in 1984 in Hong Kong where he currently lives. Wong studied multimedia design at Curtin University, Perth in 2005, after which he returned to Hong Kong to begin a career in broadcasting. He founded Wong Ping Animation Lab in 2014. His work has been exhibited in the New Museum, New York (2021, 2018); SCAD Museum of Art, Savannah (2020); Institute of Contemporary Art, Miami (2019); Camden Arts Centre, London (2019); Kunsthalle Basel (2019); Today Art Museum, Beijing (2018); and the 6th Athens Biennial (2018).

Hoping for a Good Life Everybody is Exhausted

Bahar Sayed

My friend and I spoke about trust when I unknowingly relocated. As we lay side by side, she or I convincing me or her that the very first thing we do as humans, the act of being born, is an act of trust.

We trust, it has been said, that humans require meaningful connections to maintain a sense of wellbeing, that life is influenced by our ability to practice safe intimacy and vulnerability. Yet our first commitment is forced into the hands of others presuming to guide and guard.

Holding to this myth, trying for trusting in trust – its pantomimes meaningless in repetition and exhausted by practice – becomes the foundation for a world of fractured communities, stressed societies. Displaced, separated, long distance, and misplaced. Marching under the flag bearing the words: 'WE ARE ALL IN THIS TOGETHER', we continue to maintain civility and contribute to the performance of order whilst feeling unsupported in the face of current disasters, and totally ill-equipped to deal with the impending catastrophes.

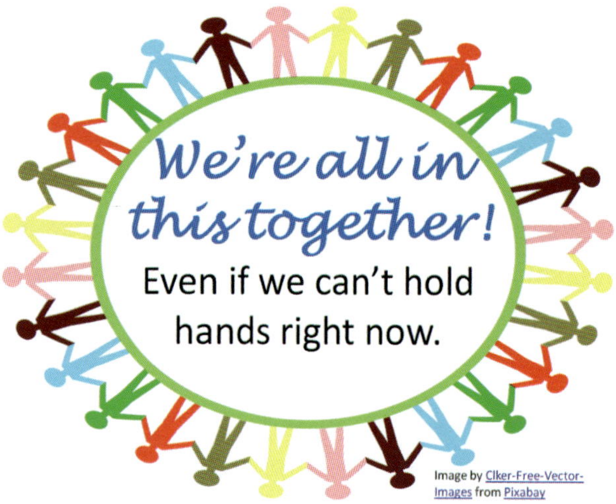

Image by Clker-Free-Vector-Images from Pixabay

Healthy living through unprecedented times, I knowingly isolate and am reintroduced to the suburbs. That's not to say that I had forgotten the buffalo grass, the dads receding to their half-open garages, and the constant rush of the distant highway irregularly pierced with bird calls. I trust it was and will be here all along, but to see it – lying on this side, the removed side – answers for that lost feeling of reunion.

The suburbs are host sites unconcerned with recollection. I trust we were isolated before we were isolating. With spaces perfectly poised between real moments of purity and the non-experiences of banality, I impress on myself to become self-abandoned and wholly obliged by family and poorly maintained routine phone calls with friends and consistent commenting with vapid admiration on acquaintances' Instagram posts; and my lack of intention and consideration quickly begins to show. Dehydrated by empty attempts at sustaining connection, I am thirsting to mouth that I live here and live there and cannot get back and cannot leave here, and there was a takeover there and a takeover here and...

I joke with a friend, a friend who is more family, 'I feel nothing yet I still love you'. She returns with a passage: 'to understand just one life, you have to swallow the world'.

She never tells me the name of the book and my sister once told me our skin is the barrier to collective empathy.

Later I asked her for details of the study and she said the skin functions as an affective barrier between the organism and its environment. This barrier reminds us where we end and another begins. With this separation, we are able to distinguish when pain is happening to you and what pain is happening to me. It is what stops us from spilling into each other. In place of stats she shared poetics. She had actually forgotten the data in the study.

My hunch on love is a yearning for osmosis, a border crossing, a desire for the skin's permeability to weaken so that all I contain can transfuse with that which makes you whole. I'm aware that I have not applied the science correctly, and, given the current teachings on personal boundaries, this is not an appropriate remedy to the feeling of isolation.

Be Fluid. Hold no fixed shape. Yielding easily to external pressures, I didn't stop to consider what forms of care I have to offer or if they are forms that hold or leak. To know this would require (self) reflection. Instructed across religious, pop-psych, and social wellness messaging, the willingness to (self)evaluate is crucial to any process of connection. Before connecting with others, we must be in communion with ourselves, making the most of our solitude by reflecting deeply and exploring new sensitivities. Ordered inside my body to mark the contours, forging form and defining boundaries, I fear that my edges will be unwelcoming and sharp. Perhaps my chalice hollow. It's safer to continue my habits in another vessel than it is to carve out space within my own. This is the statistic where one and one add up to one.

Claudia Rankine defends my disposition for this kind of single living:

> It occurs to me that feelings fill the gaps created by the indirectness of experience. Though the experience is social, thoughts carry into a singular space and it is this that causes the feelings of loneliness; or it is this that collides the feeling with the experience so that what is left is the solitude called loneliness. [1]

Claudia Rankine, *Don't Let Me Be Lonely* (Minnesota: Graywolf Press, 2004), 89.

Lonely and pulled into a multitude of directions across barriers, boundaries and borders. Connection is negotiated across the sites which label our very separation and in the saying of which borders are essentialised and fixed. I know because, in truth, I am a place where borders are continuously constructed, de-constructed, and re-constructed. Borders are not a representation of pre-existing differences between people and places, they are sites of multiple tensions on which we negotiate our separations. As lines on maps or the barriers between you and me, the suburb, a city, Father, One, they are a tool to assert order or a potential for alternative forms of engagement.

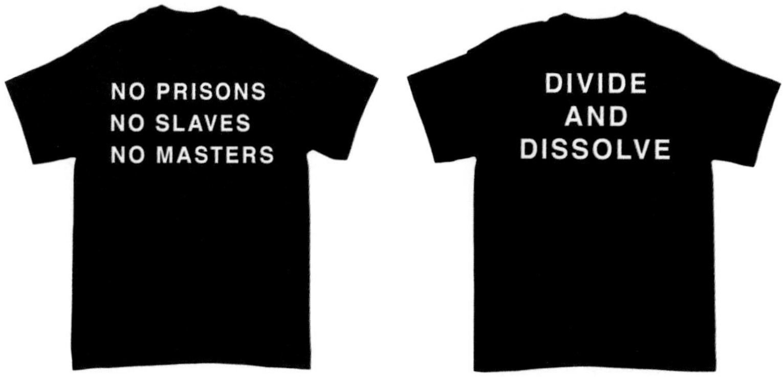

(Divide and Dissolve, T-shirt merchandise)

As a tool to tell us how to fear for public good, in fear of the coronavirus pandemic, the Australian government extended its harsh borders, once directed at refugees, asylum seekers and the poor, onto its very own citizens. Relying on isolation, Fortress Australia congratulated itself while global death tolls rose, exposing the cruelty inherent in our governing structures. The celebration was a demonstration that life does not matter and our exhaustion was deepened with the recognition that millions of lives never mattered. Alone, we grieve the worldwide heartbreak.

> Too scarred by hope to hope, too experienced to experience, too close to dead is what I think.[2]

2. Ibid, 23.

Hopelessness has diminished and eroded the possibility of meaningful and caring connections. In its place we form intimacy without risk and seek pleasures without significant emotional investment. Rankine helps make sense of this exhaustion, admitting:

> [t]his new tendency might be indicative of a deepening personality flaw: IMH, The Inability to Maintain Hope, which translates into no innate trust in the supreme laws that govern us.[3]

3. Ibid.

In my desperate attempts for connection, the energy spent trying to escape my body is used as a distraction from (self)reflection. I crawl up, I spill out, I'm tired and shy, *please can you hold me?* The exposure has done little to cure the feeling of isolation, nor has spilling guts worked to bring you any closer.

bell hooks calls me out on this, '[i]t is far easier to talk about loss than it is to talk about love. It is easier to articulate the pain of love's absence than to describe its presence and meaning in our lives.'[4] Intimacy is regarded as the best therapy for the pain of disconnection. In intimacy we explicitly share our deeper nature with each other in the belief that we can be fully known and trust that we will be accepted. When we reveal ourselves and find that this brings healing rather than harm, we make

4. bell hooks, *all about love* (New York: HarperCollins, 2001), XXVI.

John Welwood, *Love and Awakening: Discovering the Sacred Path of Intimate Relationship* (New York: HarperCollins, 1997), 142.

an important discovery – that meaningful relationships can provide a sanctuary from the world of facades.[5]

The preaching is for radical intimacy reduced to 'know yourself so you can know others'. Confronted by the first step, I am no longer interested in what I have declared I am seeking. My call for connection is worthless when I am willing only to shift shape to have you fit. You doesn't matter, *without me* does. You are the escape.

A year or so later, while moving through my reluctance to call my current location a home, the theory on trust was expanded with another friend. Over the phone, across lockdowns and hard borders, we discussed how the act of being born is an experience of stress and violence. Expelled from an immersive warmth and pushed into a world of barriers, it is the first experience of separation. Still, we agreed that trusting is not naive.

The publication BODIED is linked to the exhibition BODIED at The Art Gallery of Western Australia, Perth, from 19 December 2020 to 1 March 2021. It is the first title in the publication series 'Unclaimed Ideas' published by AGWA and SLF ICAA.

This publication was made possible thanks to the financial support of the Simon Lee Foundation and The Art Gallery of Western Australia Foundation.

Curated by Rachel Ciesla and Robert Cook

Editors: Rachel Ciesla and Robert Cook
Authors: Rachel Ciesla, Lead Creative, Simon Lee Foundation, AGWA
Robert Cook, Curator, AGWA
Ian McLean, Hugh Ramsey Chair of Australian Art History, University of Melbourne
Bahar Sayed, Curatorial Assistant, AGWA

Copy Editor: Kay Campbell, The Comma Institute

Design: Ruolan Xi (@unax.lab) and Marco Dalle Fratte (@marcodallefratte)

Artwork photography: Bo Wong

Installation views: Robert Frith – Acorn Photo

Printed in Australia by Scotts

Published and distributed by
The Art Gallery of Western Australia
Simon Lee Foundation Institute of Contemporary Asian Art
Mousse Publishing

The Art Gallery of Western Australia
PO Box 8363, Perth Business Centre
Perth, Western Australia 6849
T + 61 8 9492 6600
admin@artgallery.wa.gov.au
artgallery.wa.gov.au

Mousse Publishing
Contrappunto s.r.l.
Via Pier Candido Decembrio 28,
20137, Milan-Italy

Available through:

Mousse Publishing, Milan
moussemagazine.it

DAP | Distributed Art Publishers, New York
artbook.com

Les presses du réel, Dijon
lespressesdureel.com

Antenne Books, London
antennebooks.com

First edition: 2022
ISBN: 978-0-6481062-4-1 (The Art Gallery of Western Australia) /
978-88-6749-536-8 (Mousse Publishing)
€ 22 / $ 25

The essay by Ian McLean on Gordon Bennett 'Shadow Time' is reprinted, with permission, from the exhibition catalogue by Christopher Chapman, 1996 *Adelaide Biennial of Australian Art* (Adelaide: Art Gallery Board of South Australia, 1996).